Nuffield Primary Science
SCIENCE PROCESSES AND CONCEPT EXPLORATION

Light

Ages
7-12

TEACHERS' GUIDE

PUBLISHED FOR THE NUFFIELD–CHELSEA CURRICULUM TRUST BY COLLINS EDUCATIONAL

NUFFIELD PRIMARY SCIENCE
Science Processes and Concept Exploration

Directors
Paul Black
Wynne Harlen

Deputy Director
Terry Russell

Project members
Robert Austin
Derek Bell
Adrian Hughes
Ken Longden
John Meadows
Linda McGuigan
Jonathan Osborne
Pamela Wadsworth
Dorothy Watt

First published 1993 by Collins Educational
An imprint of HarperCollins*Publishers*
77-85 Fulham Palace Road
London W6 8JB

Second edition published 1995
Reprinted 1996

ISBN 0 00 310256 4

Printed and bound by Scotprint Ltd, Musselburgh

Design by Carla Turchini, Chi Leung
Illustrations by John Booth, Mike Dodd, Maureen
Hallahan, Rhian Nest-James, Guy Smith, Karen Tushingham,
Jakki Wood
Cover artwork by Karen Tushingham

Photograph acknowledgements
Page 28-9: Rex Features
Page 50: Hutchison Library
Page 73: Mary Evans Picture Library
Page 78: Zefa

Commissioned photography by Oliver Hatch

The Trust and the Publishers would like to thank the
governors, staff and pupils of Hillbrook Primary School,
Tooting, for their kind co-operation with many of the
photographs in this book.

Safety adviser
Peter Borrows

Other contributors
Elizabeth Harris
Carol Joyes
Anne de Normanville
Ralph Hancock

Contents

Explanation of symbols in the margins

 Warning

 Good opportunities to develop and assess work related to Experimental and Investigative Science

 Notes which may be useful to the teacher

 Vocabulary work

 Opportunities for children to use information technology

 Equipment needed

 Reference to the pupils' books

CHAPTER 1

Introduction

1.1 The SPACE approach to teaching and learning science

A primary class where the SPACE approach to science is being used may not at first seem different from any other class engaged in science activities; in either, children will be mentally and physically involved in exploring objects and events in the world around them. However, a closer look will reveal that both the children's activities and the teacher's role differ from those found in other approaches. The children are not following instructions given by others; they are not solving a problem set them by someone else. They are deeply involved in work which is based on their own ideas, and they have taken part in deciding how to do it.

The teacher has, of course, prepared carefully to reach the point where children try out their ideas. She or he will have started on the topic by giving children opportunities to explore from their own experience situations which embody important scientific ideas. The teacher will have ensured that the children have expressed their ideas about what they are exploring, using one or more of a range of approaches – from whole class discussion to talking with individual children, or asking children to write or draw – and will have explored the children's reasons for having those ideas.

With this information the teacher will have decided how to help the children to develop or revise their ideas. That may involve getting the children to use the ideas to make a prediction, then testing it by seeing if it works in practice; or the children may gather further evidence to discuss and think about. In particular, the teacher will note how 'scientific' children have been in their gathering and use of evidence; and should, by careful questioning, encourage greater rigour in the use of scientific process skills.

It is essential that the children change their ideas only as a result of what they find themselves, not by merely accepting ideas which they are told are better.

By carefully exploring children's ideas, taking them seriously and choosing appropriate ways of helping the children to test them, the teacher can move children towards ideas which apply more widely and fit the evidence better – those which are, in short, more scientific.

You will find more information about the SPACE approach in the Nuffield Primary Science *Science Co-ordinators' handbook*.

1.2 Useful strategies

Finding out children's ideas

This guide points out many opportunities for finding out children's ideas. One way is simply by talking, but there are many others. We have found the following strategies effective. How you use them may depend on the area of science you are dealing with. In Chapter 3 you will find examples of these strategies. More information about them is given in the *Science Co-ordinators' handbook*.

Talking and open questioning

Whole class discussions can be useful for sharing ideas, but they do not always give all children a chance to speak. It is often helpful if children are allowed to think of their own ideas first, perhaps working them out in drawings, and are then encouraged to share these with others – perhaps with just one other child, or with a larger group.

Annotated drawings

Asking children to draw their ideas can give a particularly clear insight into what they think. It also gives you a chance to discuss the children's ideas with them. Words conveying these ideas can then be added to the drawing, either by you or by the child. Such work can be kept as a permanent record.

Sorting and classifying

This can be a useful way of helping children to clarify their ideas and to record their thinking. They could sort a collection of objects or pictures into groups.

Writing down ideas

Children may instead write down their responses to questions you pose. Writing gives children the opportunity to express their own views, which can then be shared with others or investigated further.

Log books and diaries

These can be used to record changes over a longer investigation. They need not necessarily be kept by individual children, but could be kept by a whole group or class. Children can jot down their ideas, as words or drawings, when they notice changes, recording their reasons for what they observe.

Helping children to develop their ideas

Letting children test their own ideas

This will involve children in using some or all of the process skills of science:

- observing
- measuring
- hypothesizing
- predicting
- planning and carrying out fair tests
- interpreting results and findings
- communicating

It is an important strategy which can, and should, be used often. The *use* of process skills *develops* them – for example, through greater attention to detail in observing, more careful control of variables in fair tests, and taking all the evidence into account in interpreting the results.

Encouraging generalization from one context to another

Does an explanation proposed for a particular event fit one which is not exactly the same, but which involves the same scientific concept? You or the children might suggest other contexts that might be tried. This might be done by discussing the evidence for and against the explanation, or by gathering more evidence and testing the idea in the other context, depending on children's familiarity with the events being examined.

Discussing the words children use to describe their ideas

Children can be asked to be quite specific about the meaning of words they use, whether scientific or not. They can be prompted to think of alternative words which have almost the same meaning. They can discuss, where appropriate, words which have special meaning in a scientific context, and so be helped to realize the difference between the 'everyday' use of some words and the scientific one.

Extending the range of evidence

Some of the children's ideas may be consistent with the evidence at present available to them, but could be challenged by extending the range of evidence. This applies particularly to things which are not easily observed, such as slow changes; or those which are normally hidden, such as the insides of objects. Attempts to make these imperceptible things perceptible, often by using secondary sources, help children to consider a wider range of evidence.

Getting children to communicate their ideas

Expressing ideas in any way – through writing, drawing, modelling or, particularly, through discussion – involves thinking them through, and often rethinking and revising them. Discussion has a further advantage in that it is two-way and children can set others' ideas against their own. Just realizing that there are different ideas helps them to reconsider their own.

1.3 Equal opportunities

The SPACE approach to teaching and learning science gives opportunities for every child to build on and develop his or her experiences, skills and ideas. It can therefore be used to benefit pupils of all kinds and at any stage of development. This is fully discussed in the *Science Co-ordinators' handbook*.

1.4 Light and the curriculum

This teachers' guide is divided into three themes; in each one there is a section on finding out children's ideas, examples of ideas children have, and a section on helping children to develop their ideas.

Light sources and vision

This theme indicates ways in which children might be helped to develop their ideas about light sources, vision and the representation of light.

In the activities suggested for developing children's ideas about light sources, the children explore their surroundings for light sources, compare light sources, and discuss illumination. Through these investigations children may come to an understanding of the differences between a primary and a secondary light source.

Specific activities associated with vision are not suggested; however, children will need to consider how they see objects in many of the activities in this theme. Through discussion, observation, and comparing ideas about vision, children may become aware that we see primary sources because light travels directly to our eye, whereas light is reflected to the eye by secondary sources. Many children find the ideas associated with secondary sources difficult at Key Stage 2, and further activities in the theme 'Reflections and shadows' may be helpful.

Throughout this theme there are opportunities for children to develop the idea that light travels and that light can be represented as straight line rays.

Reflections and shadows

This theme indicates ways in which children might be helped to develop their ideas about reflection, reflected images, and shadows.

Children may confuse shadows with reflections. They may be more aware of light reflected by shiny and mirror surfaces than dull surfaces, and not fully understand that all secondary surfaces reflect light.

In the activities suggested for developing children's ideas about reflection, children observe reflected images and reflection by mirrors, and investigate reflection of light in the context of road safety and signalling. Observation of light reflected by mirrors may lead children to explore angular patterns and symmetry.

Some of the activities in which children observe and explore the formation of shadows caused by the Sun may also help them to understand the Sun's daily movement across the sky. By exploring opaque, transparent and translucent materials children may come to an understanding that light travels through some materials and not others. Children may observe refraction effects during these investigations, but there are no activities for developing children's ideas on refraction.

Colour

This theme indicates ways in which children might be helped to develop their ideas about colour.

Children may be aware of the bright and dominant colours in our environment, that colours can be used to warn us, and that certain colours help us identify people and places. However, they may not be aware of the full significance of colour in our daily lives.

In the activities for developing children's ideas about colour, children explore the significance of colour in the natural and built environment. They can investigate colour change by mixing paints, by looking through filters, and by mixing reflected light with colour spinners. The effect of colour on our mood, preference and choice can be explored and discussed.

Many of the activities may help children to widen their experience in the uses of colour, and the investigations may help them to develop their exploratory skills. A scientific understanding of colour is not required at Key Stage 2 and there are no activities to develop this understanding.

(See note on page 79.)

National Curriculum Programmes of Study	Environmental Studies 5-14 (Scotland): Science
Physical Processes **3 Light and sound** **a** that light travels from a source; **d** that we see light sources because light from them enters our eyes.	**Understanding Energy and Forces (Stages P4 to P6)** **Properties and uses of energy** • mirrors and reflections, including curved mirrors; • lenses.
Physical Processes **3 Light and sound** **b** that light cannot pass through some materials, and that this leads to the formation of shadows; **c** that light is reflected from surfaces.	**Understanding Energy and Forces (Stages P4 to P6)** **Properties and uses of energy** • sunlight and shadows; • simple applications of mirrors and lenses.
Colour appears in the Art National Curriculum at Key Stage 2, not science. Pupils should be taught how colour is applied and to identify how it is used in images and artefacts for different purposes (Ar4b, 8e, 9b).	**Understanding Energy and Forces (Stages P4 to P6)** **Properties and uses of energy** • colours in sunlight, visible spectrum formed by a prism.

1.5 Experimental and Investigative Science

Two important aspects of children's learning in science are:

◆ learning how to investigate the world around them;
◆ learning to make sense of the world around them using scientific ideas.

These are reflected in the National Curriculum. 'Experimental and Investigative Science' covers the first aspect. The second aspect is covered by the rest of the Programme of Study. Although these two aspects of science learning are separated in the National Curriculum they cannot be separated in practice and it is not useful to try to do so. Through investigation children explore their ideas and/or test out the ideas which arise from discussion. As a result, ideas may be advanced, but this will depend on the children's investigation skills. Thus it is important to develop these skills in the context of activities which extend ideas. So there is no separate Nuffield Primary Science teachers' guide on scientific investigations, because opportunities to make these occur throughout all the guides and they form an essential part of the SPACE approach.

Thus in this guide you will find investigations which provide opportunities to develop and assess the skills and understanding set out in Experimental and Investigative Science. These are marked in the text by the symbol shown here. In this teachers' guide, the investigations which cover the most skills are 'Identifying and grouping light sources' (page 41), 'Using mirrors and reflectors' (page 63), 'Which materials and shapes make the best reflectors?' (page 63), 'Shadows of objects' (page 72), and 'Road Safety' (page 84).

It is important that teachers give active guidance to pupils during investigations to help them work out how to improve the way in which they plan and carry out their investigations.

Experimental and Investigative Science is about the ways scientific evidence can be obtained, about the ways observations and measurements are made, and about the way in which the evidence is analysed. It therefore sets out three main ways in which pupils can develop their ability to do experimental and investigative science, as follows:-

1 'Planning experimental work'. Here, children should be helped to make progress from asking general and vague questions, to suggesting ideas which could be tested. Teachers' discussion with pupils should aim to help them to make predictions, using their existing understanding, on the basis of which they can decide what evidence should be collected. This should lead them to think about what apparatus and equipment they should use.

When children describe plans for their work, they should be helped to think about what features they are going to change, what effects of these changes they are going to observe or measure, and what features they must keep the same. In this way they can come to understand what is meant by 'a fair test'.

2 'Obtaining evidence'. Children should make observations in the light of their ideas about what they are looking for and why. When they describe their observations, teachers may have to help them to improve, for example by reminding them of their original aims and plan for the work. Such help should also encourage progress from qualitative comparisons and judgements to appreciating the value of making quantitative measurements (for example 'cold water' is qualitative, 'water at 12°C' is quantitative). This should lead to the development of skills with a variety of instruments and to increasing care and accuracy in measurement, involving, for example, repeating measurements to check.

3 'Considering evidence'. Here, children should first learn to record their evidence in systematic and clear ways, starting with simple drawings and then learning to use tables, bar charts and line graphs to display the patterns in numerical data. Then they should be asked to think about and discuss their results, considering what might be learnt from any trends or patterns. As ideas develop, they should be careful in checking their evidence against the original idea underlying the investigation and should become increasingly critical in discussing alternative explanations which might fit their evidence. In such discussions, they should be helped to relate their arguments to their developing scientific understanding. They should also be guided to see possibilities for conducting their investigation more carefully, or in quite different ways.

Whilst these three may seem to form a natural sequence of stages, children's work might not follow this particular sequence. For example, some might start with evidence from their observations and proceed on this basis to propose a hypothesis and a plan to test it. For others, the results of one task may be the starting point for a new inquiry involving new measurements. Useful learning about how to investigate might arise when only one or two of the above aspects of an investigation are involved, or when the teacher tells children about some aspects so that they can concentrate on others. However, there should be some occasions for all pupils when they carry out the whole process of investigation by themselves.

The assessment examples given in chapter 4 are analysed in relation to the level descriptions, which describe children's progress in relation to these three aspects: *planning experimental work, obtaining evidence* and *considering evidence*. Thus, these three provide a framework both for guiding children and for assessing their progress in experimental and investigative work.

CHAPTER 2

Planning

2.1 Introduction: planning with children's ideas in mind

The key scientific ideas presented in this guide can be explored in various contexts, and many of the suggested activities can be incorporated into cross-curricular topic work. This chapter uses a worked example as an aid to planning a topic. Further information on planning is given in the *Science Co-ordinators' handbook*.

A teacher using the SPACE approach should take into account:

◆ the need to find out children's own ideas, not only at the beginning of the work but also at intervals during it;
◆ the importance of planning the investigations with the children, using their ideas as the starting point;
◆ the concepts that are being explored;
◆ the direction in which the children's ideas are developing.

2.2 Cross-curricular topics

Activities which explore the ideas covered in this teachers' guide to *Light* may be approached via a number of topics in addition to the one set out as an example in the planning sheets (pages 15–16). It is assumed that teachers will adapt the topic to whatever local resources are of interest and readily to hand. Some possibilities are given below.

Patterns

Patterns of reflected light at various mirror surfaces, and at mirrors set at angles.
Making a kaleidoscope.
Symmetrical patterns in Rangoli, Islamic, or Palestinian traditional designs, among others.
The pattern of colours in the spectrum of white light could be introduced.
Painting the patterns seen in the structure of leaves, plants and fossils or in snow crystals, giving experience in colour mixing.
Filters could be used to produce patterns of coloured light.
Children could explore patterns in shadow, indoors and outside.
Observing movement of shadows in sunlight could lead to a study of patterns in the Solar System, stars and seasonal patterns including changes in animal and human behaviour patterns, and weather patterns.
Time lines, log books, and diaries could reveal patterns in human activities and celebrations over time.

Some links with other Nuffield Primary Science teachers' guides and pupils' books include:

The Earth in Space – the Solar System, seasonal change;
Rocks, soil and weather – patterns in the weather at different times of the year.

Signs and signals

Colour, vision, reflection and a study of light sources.
Ways of sending signals and messages. Activities might include finding out about suitable light sources to send messages, directing light by reflection, a consideration of how light travels, designing circuits to control light sources and alarms. Sound as a means of signalling could also be considered.
Ways in which colours, reflectors and reflective surfaces help to warn and keep us safe. Comparing the visibility of colours and surfaces would develop children's investigative skills and encourage them to think about vision.

Some links with other Nuffield Primary Science teachers' guides and pupils' books include:

Sound and music – sound as a means of signalling and sending messages; alarms and signals;
Electricity and magnetism – making electric circuits.

Festivals

Festivals and celebrations such as Divali, Hannukah, Eid, Easter, Christmas and Harvest Festival may serve as a focus for work on light.
Light sources used in festivals.
Design decorations and decorative lights.
Enact some of the stories associated with those festivals, showing them with shadow puppets, or as illuminated displays and dioramas.
Aspects of the Solar System and seasonal change associated with some of the celebrations, together with the significance of the colours used in the traditional dress.

Some links with other Nuffield Primary Science teachers' guides and pupils' books include:

Electricity and magnetism – making electric circuits;
The Earth in Space – the Solar System and seasonal change.

Around our school

This topic could include much of the work on warning signs, signals and safety already suggested in the topic 'Signs and signals'.
Lighting in the school, roadway and shops.
Colour in decoration, clothing and advertising.
Shadows in familiar places indoors and outside.
Some of the work suggested in 'Festivals' could also be incorporated in this topic by considering the decorations, customs and artefacts of different cultural groups in the school and the community.

2.3 Topic plan examples

The plans on pages 15 and 16 illustrate how the science related to *Light* may be embedded in a cross-curricular topic. The topic presented is 'Signals and Signs' and opportunities for exploring mathematics, language, history, geography, design, technology and art have been indicated on the first plan. On the second plan the science work has been amplified to illustrate possible areas of exploration based within the overall topic. It is important to remember these are only examples and are not intended to be exhaustive.

2.4 Use of information technology

 Specific examples of opportunities to use information technology are indicated by this symbol in the margin and referred to in the text.

Information technology could be used to record work using a word processor, and to show results such as types of light sources or colours found on local buildings in a graph.

2.5 Pupils' books

The pupils' books accompanying this guide are called *Light* for the lower juniors and *More About Light* for the upper juniors. The pupils' books are intended to be used spread by spread. The spreads are not sequential, and they are covered in these notes in thematic order.

Features of the pupils' books include:
◆ Stimulus spreads, often visual, designed to raise questions, arouse curiosity, and to promote discussion.

◆ Information spreads, which give secondary source material in a clear and attractive way.

◆ Activity ideas, to form the basis of investigations to be carried out by the children.

◆ Cross-curricular spreads and stories which can act as a basis for creative writing, or spreads with a historical or creative focus.

◆ Real life examples of applications of science in the everyday world.

Light

Look at me pages 2–3

Purpose: To prompt an open-ended discussion about eyes, including 'eye patterns'.
Notes: The eyes on page 2 are: tree frog, cat, bushbaby, fox and barn owl – all animals which are active at night.
Extension activity: Children could draw their own eyes and make eye patterns.
Teachers' guide cross-reference: Light, page 48.

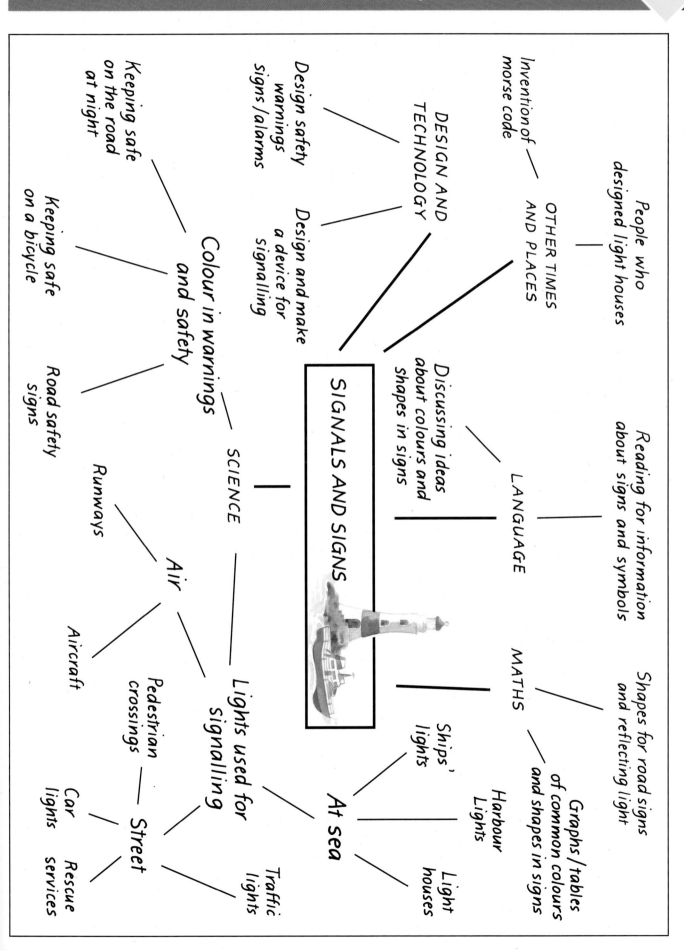

SIGNALS AND SIGNS

OTHER TIMES AND PLACES
People who designed light houses
Invention of morse code

DESIGN AND TECHNOLOGY
Design safety warnings signs / alarms
Design and make a device for signalling

LANGUAGE
Discussing ideas about colours and shapes in signs
Reading for information about signs and symbols

MATHS
Shapes for road signs and reflecting light
Graphs / tables of common colours and shapes in signs

At sea
Ships' lights
Harbour Lights
Light houses

SCIENCE
Colour in warnings and safety
Keeping safe on the road at night
Keeping safe on a bicycle
Road safety signs

Lights used for signalling
Air
Runways
Aircraft
Pedestrian crossings
Street
Traffic lights
Car lights
Rescue services

15

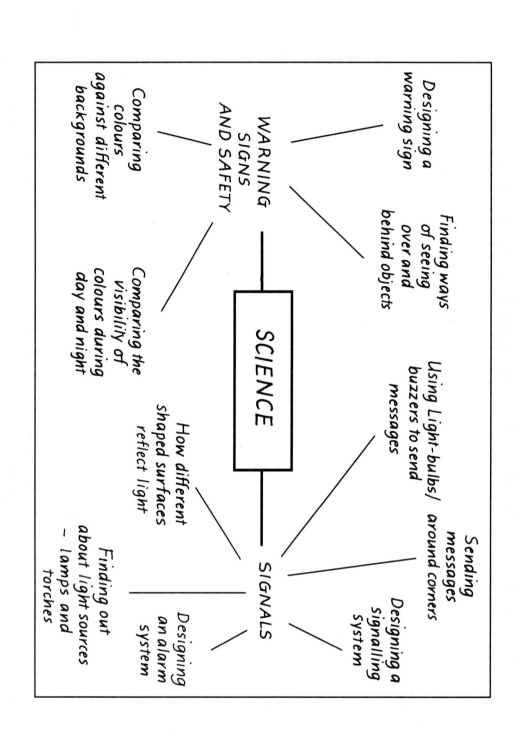

How eyes work pages 10–11

Purpose: To provide support for a discussion about how eyes work.
Note: The tear gland – actually inside the eyelid – is shown at the top right-hand side of the large picture of the eye.
Teachers' guide cross-references: Light, pages 46-7, 106-7.

I don't believe my eyes! pages 20–21

Purpose: To introduce the idea that eyes can 'play tricks' and that vision is related to perception.
Extension activity: Try the colour-blindness test on pages 8–9 of *More about light.*
Teachers' guide cross-reference: Light, page 48.

Making pictures with light pages 14–15

Purpose: To explain that a camera needs light to work.
Notes: The film in a camera is coated with chemicals, which react to the light from the lens, and the picture forms. The chemicals used in early photographs worked slowly. Modern chemicals only need a fraction of a second. The activity described on page 14 needs bright sunlight to get a quick result.
Idea for discussion: Compare the formal pose of the Victorian/Edwardian family with the casual pose of the modern picture. Can the children suggest reasons for this contrast? (Possibilities include the speed of the camera shutter, whether or not photographs were often taken, and social attitudes.)
Extension activity: Children could use a camera and take their own photographs. If the school has a darkroom, show how light and darkness are used in processing film.
Teachers' guide cross-references: Light, pages 49, 108.

Shadows pages 16–17

Purpose: To be a starting point for a discussion about shadows.
Questions for discussion: Referring to the photographs that show shadows only, ask children, what object they think made the shadow. In what ways is the shadow different from its object?
Teachers' guide cross-references: Light, pages 53-4, 69.

Shadow play pages 4–5

Purpose: To introduce the variety of shadows.
Notes: You could introduce the words 'opaque' and 'translucent'. The Indonesian puppet is opaque (light does not pass through it). The Turkish puppet is translucent, and casts a coloured shadow.
Extension activity: Children could make their own shadow puppets.
Teachers' guide cross-references: Light, pages 69, 74-76.

Mirror images pages 6–7

Purpose: To encourage children to learn more about reflections, and that these are different from shadows.
Note: For safety, use plastic mirrors.
Extension activity: Children can experiment with mirrors and small objects.
Teachers' guide cross-references: Light, pages 63, 104-5.

Reflections: seeing behind, around, under pages 22–23

Purpose: To extend discussion of the uses of mirrors.
Notes: The shopkeeper can see much more of the shop in a curved mirror. 'Catseyes' are reflectors, with no light of their own.
Extension activity: Children could collect their own reflective surfaces.
Teachers' guide cross-reference: Light, pages 63-4.

Who's there? pages 18–19

Purpose: Further discussion and investigation of reflections.
Notes: You could introduce the words concave (curved in) and convex (curved out).
Extension activity: Children can look for curved reflections in a variety of surfaces.
Teachers' guide cross-references: Light, pages 63-5, 104-6.

Choosing colours pages 12–13

Purpose: To introduce a discussion about different colours.
Extension activities: Ask children what uses they associate with the other colours shown. The children could draw their own colour wheels. Consider inviting School Works to your school – they have travelling exhibitions. (School Works, Science Projects, 20 St James Street, London W6 9RW, telephone 0181 741 7437.)
Teachers' guide cross-references: Light, pages 80, 86.

Light and colour for celebrations pages 8–9

Purpose: To introduce a discussion on the uses of light and colour in different cultures.
Note: There may be children in class who will not relate to the religions on the page.
Extension activity: Children could draw candles, or light short, stubby ones (make sure they take care – night lights are safer).
Teachers' guide cross-reference: Light, page 13.

More about light

Lighthouses pages 2–3

Purpose: To illustrate a practical application of light.
Note: The different flashing patterns identify which lighthouse the ship is approaching.
Questions for discussion: Which pictures tell you how lighthouses used to be? Which ones tell you how lighthouses are now? What is the main purpose of a lighthouse?
Teachers' guide cross-references: Light, pages 13, 15, 16, 44, 100.

Using light pages 22–23

Purpose: To increase children's awareness of how light is used in everyday situations; to illustrate further practical applications of using light; and to provide a discussion activity and an opportunity for reading for information.
Extension activity: Link with work on electricity. Children could make a poster of their own about the uses of light.
Teachers' guide cross-references: Light, pages 13, 15, 45, 100-1.

Putting light on paper pages 16–17

Purpose: To introduce the representation of light, providing a link to art and design and to media studies; and to provide an English activity (thinking of words to describe light).
Extension activities: Visit an art gallery (try to arrange for an education officer to show you round) and look out for pictures in which light is represented. Look for further examples in pictures and books. Encourage children to draw their own cartoon images of light and to paint still-life pictures incorporating light and shade. Suggest that children take their own photographs showing light and shade.
Teachers' guide cross-references: Light, pages 12, 30, 36, 46, 104.

Look and listen pages 20–21

Purpose: To point out that there are everyday expressions based on vision and that the literal meaning of these can run counter to scientific fact.
Extension activity: Not all the expressions on these pages are illustrated. Children could provide their own pictures for those for which there are none.
Pupils' book cross-references: More about sound and music pages 10-11.
Teachers' guide cross-references: Light, pages 34, 38-40, 46-7.

Making moving pictures pages 12–13

Purpose: An activity spread, to explain how film works.
Extension activities: Arrange a visit to a media museum such as the Museum of the Moving Image London, (telephone 0171 401 2636) or The National Museum of Photography, Film and Television, Pictureville, Bradford BD1 1NQ, (telephone 01274 727488); or a toy museum, such as The Bethnal Green Museum of Childhood London, (telephone 0181 980 2415).
Teachers' guide cross-reference: Light, page 49.

Signalling pages 10–11

Purpose: To give children more exposure to the various uses of light, colour and reflection and to introduce ideas about the country code, fires, safety.
Extension activity: Children could discuss the various ways they know of attracting attention.
Teachers' guide cross-references: Light, pages 13, 15, 16, 65.

Cycling to school pages 14–15

Purpose: To summarize features of light, including colour and reflection.
Note: In the final picture the child is removing the bicycle's safety equipment, as an anti-theft device.
Questions for discussion: Encourage children to discuss and list all the safety devices the child in the picture uses. Point out that many of these features are vital as, even in daylight, it is difficult to see a child in a dark school uniform.
Extension activities: Children could write their own story captions to go with the pictures. They could sort the devices under the headings: reflectors, colour, light.
Teachers' guide cross-references: Light, pages 13, 15, 16, 52, 64-5, 67.

Look again pages 18–19

Purpose: A teacher-led discussion spread designed to follow up the work on reflections in *Light*. It aims to help define the distinction between shadow and reflection.
Notes: The tree photograph is actually upside down.
Teachers' guide cross-references: Light, pages 12–3, 52–3, 61, 67.

Colours and feelings pages 4–5

Purpose: To encourage children to consider expressions in which colours are used to evoke emotions.
Extension activities: Children could design a new colour scheme for a chosen room (a bedroom, classroom etc). Children could design, or redesign, their school uniform. They could mix up a paint chart or colour palette, and make up names for their new colours. Ask them to write their own poem – linking this activity to their English language work.
Teachers' guide cross-references: Light, pages 12, 87, 89.

The effects of coloured light pages 6–7

Purpose: To provide further work on vision as perception and the idea that colour is not absolute. (It can change according to the conditions under which we see it.)
Note: In a real theatre, a green filter would be used, and not blue and yellow as shown here.
Extension activities: Children could think of their own perception of colour and how it can be changed, by wearing coloured spectacles, for example. The theatre lighting picture may lead to discussion about moods connected with different colours. Link this work to the poem on the previous spread (Colours and feelings). Children could devise their own ideas for using coloured lighting for scenes in a school play. They could carry out simple experiments with torches and coloured filters.
Teachers' guide cross-references: Light, pages 79, 87, 88-9, 101-2.

Dotty pictures pages 8–9

Purpose: To be a 'wow' spread about visual images which children may come across in their everyday experience; to encourage them to look closely at visual images from everyday experience; and to show that a television screen is made up of the three primary colours of light: red, blue, green.
Notes: Children should be warned not to touch a television screen, because of static electricity. Some children may notice for the first time that they are colour-blind.
Extension activities: Ask the children to paint their own dotty pictures. Use lenses, other viewing equipment and microscopes to look at images for dots. Visit an art gallery to look at pictures composed of dots.
Teachers' guide cross-references: Light, pages 89-90, 102.

2.6 Planning your science programme in school

The following pages give examples of how two schools have planned their science programme for the whole of Key Stage 2. Planning of this kind helps to provide continuity and progression in children's learning in science. The development of such whole school programmes is discussed more fully in the *Science Co-ordinators' Handbook*.

Each plan covers the requirements for the National Curriculum at Key Stage 2 and shows which themes in the Nuffield Primary Science Teachers' Guides have been used for planning the topic in detail by the class teacher.

Example 1 (page 23)

Based in a semi-rural area this junior school has approximately 170 children on roll. There are no mixed age groups in the school. The plan provides for overlaps in order to provide opportunities for pupils to revisit concepts and build on their previous experience.

The overall curriculum is planned around topics which are history-led in the Autumn term, science-led in the Spring term and geography-led in the Summer term. Therefore, where ever possible cross-curricular links are developed, but if this becomes contrived, then subject specific mini-topics are planned. The programme only shows the Science elements taught each term.

Example 2 (page 24)

This urban school has recently reviewed its science programme in order to help encourage progression in the concepts covered and avoid repetition of the same activities. Teachers asked for guidance but also wanted the flexibility to develop the topics in a way which was appropriate to their own class.

It was also felt that some concepts, not necessarily demanded by the National Curriculum, should be covered e.g. Seasons. Therefore, suitable topics are included in the programme.

The summer term in Year 6 is free to accommodate SATs and to allow teachers time to further develop the interests of children.

Example 1

	AUTUMN TERM	**SPRING TERM**	**SUMMER TERM**
YEAR 3	The Earth and beyond/Magnetism	All about me	Service to our homes
Nuffield Primary Science Teachers' Guide	The Earth in Space 3.1, 3.2, 3.3 Electricity and magnetism 3.4	Living processes 3.1, 3.2, 3.3 The variety of life 3.2 Light 3.1	Electricity and magnetism 3.1, 3.2, 3.3 Materials 3.1 Using energy 3.2
Programme of Study †	Sc4:4a, b, c, d; Sc4:2a	Sc2: 1a; 2a, b, e, f; Sc4:3a, d	Sc3:1a, b, c; Sc4:1a, b, c
YEAR 4	Sound and music / Mechanisms	Habitats	Built environment
Nuffield Primary Science Teachers' Guide	Sound and music 3.1, 3.2 Using energy 3.3	The variety of life 3.1 Living processes 3.4 Living things in their environment 3.1, 3.2	Materials 3.2, 3.3 Using energy 3.1
Programme of Study †	Sc4:3e, f, g; Sc4:2d, e	Sc2:1b; 3a, b, c, d; 4a; Sc3:1d	Sc3:1e; 2a, b, c, d
YEAR 5	Electricity/Starting and stopping	Structures	Earth and atmosphere/ Light
Nuffield Primary Science Teachers' Guide	Electricity and magnetism 3.2, 3.3 Forces and movement 3.1, 3.2	Materials 3.1, 3.2, 3.3 Rocks, soil and weather 3.1 The variety of life 3.3	Rocks, soil and weather 3.2 The Earth in Space 3.1, 3.2, 3.3, 3.4 Light 3.2, 3.3
Programme of Study †	Sc4:1a, b, c, d; Sc4:2b, c	Sc3:1b, d; 2f; 3a, b, c, d, e	Sc3:2e; Sc4:4a, b, c, d; Sc4:3a, b, c
YEAR 6	The human body/Keeping healthy	Forces	Our environment
Nuffield Primary Science Teachers' Guide	Living processes 3.2, 3.3 The variety of life 3.2	Forces and movement 3.1, 3.2, 3.3, 3.4 Electricity and magnetism 3.4 Using energy 3.3	Living things in their environment 3.2, 3.3, 3.4
Programme of Study †	Sc2:2c, d, g, h	Sc4:2a, b, c, d, e, f, g, h	Sc2:5a, b, c, d, e

† For the purposes of these charts the references to sections of the Programme of Study have been abbreviated as follows:
Sc2 = Life Processes and Living Things
Sc3 = Materials and their Properties
Sc4 = Physical Processes

Example 2

	AUTUMN TERM		SPRING TERM		SUMMER TERM	
YEAR 3	Earth and time	Reflections and shadows	What's under our feet?	Moving things	Variety of life	Habitats
Nuffield Primary Science Teachers' Guide	The Earth in Space 3.1, 3.2	Light 3.2	Rocks, soil and weather 3.1 Living things in their environment 3.3	Forces and movement 3.1	The variety of life 3.1	Living things in their environment 3.1
Programme of Study †	Sc4:4a, b, c, d	Sc4:3a, b, c	Sc2:5e; Sc3:1d	Sc4:2a, b, c, d, e	Sc2:1a, b; 4a	Sc2:5a, b
YEAR 4	Frictional forces	Hot and cold	Materials and their properties	Sounds	Growing	Electricity
Nuffield Primary Science Teachers' Guide	Forces and movement 3.2	Using energy 3.1	Materials 3.1	Sound and music 3.1	Living processes 3.1, 3.4	Electricity and magnetism 3.1, 3.2, 3.3
Programme of Study †	Sc4:2b, c, f, g, h	Sc3:2b, c	Sc3:1a, b, e	Sc4:3e, f	Sc2:3a, b, c, d	Sc3:1c; Sc4:1a, b, c
YEAR 5	The Earth in the Solar System	Weather and its effects	Feeding relationships	Individual variation	Light sources	Sounds travelling
Nuffield Primary Science Teachers' Guides	The Earth in Space 3.1, 3.2, 3.3	Rocks, soil and weather 3.1, 3.2	Living things in their environment 3.2, 3.3	The variety of life 3.2	Light 3.1	Sound and music 3.2
Programme of Study †	Sc4:c, d	Sc3:1d, 2e	Sc2:5c, d, e	Sc2:4a; 5a	Sc4:3a, b, c, d	Sc4:3e, f, g
YEAR 6	Forces and movement	Living processes	Electricity	Materials		
Nuffield Primary Science Teachers' Guide	Forces and movement 3.3, 3.4	Living processes 3.2, 3.3	Electricity and magnetism 3.1, 3.2, 3.3	Materials 3.2, 3.3		
Programme of Study †	Sc4:2d, e, f, g, h	Sc2:2a, b, c, d, e, f, g, h	Sc4:1c, d	Sc3:2a, b, d, f; 3a, b, c, d, e		

2.7 Resources

Full use should be made of the school grounds, other areas of the local environment which are safely accessible, and places for appropriate visits if they can be arranged. Visits must comply with LEA guidelines.

The precise nature of the resources needed at any time will, of course, depend upon the ideas that the children have and the methods of testing that they devise. However, the following list provides a general guide to the resources needed to carry out the investigations shown in this book.

The following materials and equipment would be useful for carrying out the activities described in this book.

Powerful torches
Mirrors
Coloured acetate
Candles, candle holder, sand tray
Slide projector
Overhead projector
Large cardboard boxes
Black and coloured paper
A variety of materials including some which are opaque, transparent, and translucent
Reference books, videos and other secondary source material to supplement the pupils' books

2.8 Warnings

Activities which need particular care are indicated by this symbol in the margin. Everything possible should be done to ensure the safety of the children during their investigations. You should consult any guidelines on safety published by your own Local Education Authority and, if your school or LEA is a member, by CLEAPSS. See also the Association for Science Education publication *Be safe! Some aspects of safety in school science and technology for Key Stages 1 and 2* (2nd edition, 1990). This contains more detailed advice than can be included here.

The points listed below require particular attention.

Children must be warned not to look directly at the Sun or other bright lights. It is also important that they do not use mirrors to reflect light into each others' eyes.

Sensitivity is needed because children may have some visual impairment, particularly a degree of colour-blindness. Colour-blindness is almost exclusively restricted to boys.

CHAPTER 3

Exploring light

Theme organizer
LIGHT

LIGHT SOURCES AND VISION
3.1

Light comes from a variety of sources: primary sources which give out light directly, and secondary sources, which reflect light.

Objects can be seen because they either give out light or reflect light.

Objects are seen when light enters the eye.

REFLECTIONS AND SHADOWS
3.2

The position, shape, and size of a shadow depend upon the position of the object in relation to the position of the light source.

Light travels through some materials but not through others.

Light is reflected off objects.

*Light travels in straight lines.

COLOUR
3.3

Colours in the environment often have a particular significance for plants and animals, including humans – for example, warning coloration and camouflage.

Different colours can be created by mixing coloured paints, or by using filters.

(*Asterisks indicate ideas which will be developed more fully in later key stages.)

Light sources and vision

AREAS FOR INVESTIGATION

◆ Familiar sources of light.

◆ Representations of light in drawings.

◆ Finding out more about how we see and the importance of light.

KEY IDEAS

◆ Light comes from a variety of sources: primary sources, which give out light directly, and secondary sources, which reflect light.

◆ Objects can be seen because they either give out light or reflect light.

◆ Objects are seen when light enters the eye.

A LOOK AT
light sources and vision

We see things around us because light passes from objects to our eyes. Some objects, called **primary** light sources, give out their own light; while others, called **secondary** light sources, reflect light to the eye. The light coming from a secondary source will have originated from a primary source; for example, this page is a secondary source, and it is reflecting light that may have come from a primary source such as the Sun or the filament of a light-bulb.

Light travels very quickly, so when we switch on a light-bulb a room appears to fill with light instantaneously.

In a picture, we draw straight lines to represent light travelling, and show the direction of travel with arrowheads. These lines represent light rays.

Finding out children's ideas
STARTER ACTIVITIES

Children are likely to know of many different light sources from their everyday experiences. This will make a useful starting point for work on light. They could be asked to think about how light travels from its source, and how light is represented in drawings.

1 Light sources and their representation

Some of the following questions and activities may be useful for discovering children's ideas about light sources.

a Drawing light sources

You could begin by asking the children to:

 Think of as many things as possible which give us light.

One way of doing this is to ask the children to draw as many light sources as they can think of. Get the children to represent the light in their pictures in whatever way they like. Then ask:

 Can you show where the light and shadows are in this picture?

Give the children a copy of either of the copiable sheets on the next two pages. Ask them to add to the picture to show where the light is.

Alternatively, ask the children to draw a picture of their own, for example, the classroom, their living room or their bedroom, and to show where the light is in the picture.

Practical point: it is important that the children understand that you would like them to show light wherever they think it occurs in the picture and that you are not just asking them to colour in the light-bulbs. There can be some confusion over the use of the word 'light' (as in 'Switch on the light!') which is often used to mean 'lamp'.

b Light travelling

The idea of light travelling is closely associated with light sources. If we can see a light, it must have travelled to us from a light source.

This is a difficult idea for children to understand because it is not possible actually to show how light travels, only the effects

3.1

which are produced by this happening. (However, some idea can be given by later activities – see 'How far does light travel?', page 44.)

To find out how much children understand about how light travels, some of the following activities could be used.

You could ask the children:

Q *What lights can you think of which are used as warning signals?*

The answers given may include traffic lights, lights at pedestrian crossings, lighthouses, and warning lights in cars or on electrical equipment.

For the warning to be heeded, the light needs to be seen from some distance. Implicit in this is the idea that the light needs to travel from its source to the receiver.

c Light from a candle

Light a stubby candle or night-light and stand it in a metal tray of sand in the middle of the classroom.

CHILDREN SHOULD BE SUPERVISED DURING THIS ACTIVITY

Q *How far do you think the light from the candle will go? Do you think it will go further at night?*

Give the children the opportunity to explain their ideas by asking them to draw and write down their explanations of what happens to the light from the candle. (See also 'How can you see a candle?', page 34.)

To encourage children to start thinking about their own explanations of vision, you could ask:

 How do you see a book?

Ask the children to draw a picture to explain how you can see a book, then ask them to write or talk about their drawing.

Next, ask:

 How can you see a candle?

Light a stubby candle or night-light and stand it in a metal tray of sand in the middle of a table. Ask the children to explain how they see the candle, and then to draw a picture to illustrate their explanation. They could then write their explanation next to their drawing or discuss it with other children in the class. (See also 'Light from a candle', page 33.)

Do the children explain how they can see a candle in the same way as they explain how they can see a book? They may not realize that light is involved, because the book is not a primary light source.

You could now show children a picture such as the one on the following page, and ask:

 How does the child in the picture see the clock?

Ask the children to add to the drawing to show how the child in the picture sees the clock. The children could write or talk about their drawing.

 Why can't you see in the dark?

The children could write their response before sharing it with the rest of the class.

Children's ideas

1 Ideas about light sources and their representation

The children's drawings will show the ways in which they represent light. For example, it may be:

- as a 'halo' of simple lines radiating from a light source;
- as a beam;
- as simple lines, or a complicated series of lines, representing the path of the light;
- by shading.

In addition to showing how they represent light, children's drawings may give some indication of the concepts they have. It is best not to make assumptions based solely on drawings: for example, children who represent light by drawing straight lines do not necessarily understand that light travels in straight lines. But at least drawings will show some of the observations children have made about light, and will provide useful starter activities for further work.

These pictures show the typical range of light sources drawn by children at Key Stage 2. It is common for children to add lines to their drawings to show the light radiating from the source, particularly the Sun. Children tend to show the light from torches or car headlights as a beam.

Sources of light

The drawings below were made by children in response to the instruction: Draw as many places as you can think of where light comes from.

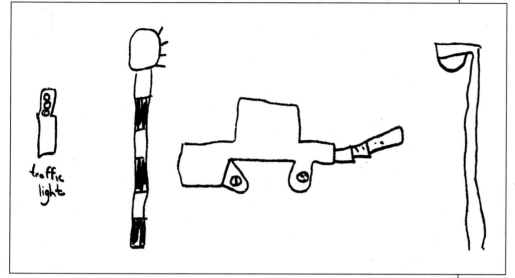

Lights seen in the streets

Lights associated with children's fiction

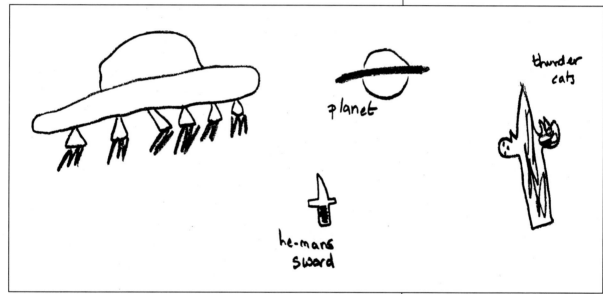

Light sources associated with fire and burning

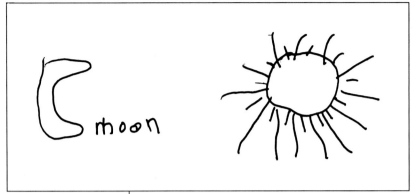

Light sources associated with the solar system

Shiny surfaces which reflect light

2 Ideas about vision

Children are usually aware that 'we see with our eyes', 'by looking', and that 'we need light'.

Few children will have an understanding of the scientific explanation of vision – that light has to enter our eyes from objects for us to see them.

Typical responses to questions about how children see a book ranged from simply drawing the book to attempting quite complex replies involving the direction in which the light was travelling. The following responses were typical:

By using your eyes!

By looking.

We can see the book because in your eyes there is a black thing and it is called a pupil and it helps you see.

These children did not mention light or recognize that this was a question requiring a scientific explanation; they explained vision simply in terms of seeing or looking. Other children do realize that light is essential for vision, but are not sure what part it plays.

Many children attempt to draw links between the light source and the eyes, particularly when they are asked to draw a picture to explain how they can see a candle. Some children give different responses to the questions about seeing the book and seeing the candle.

> *When the light is in our eyes we can read the words, but when the light is off we can't read.*

Children are often aware of light coming towards their eyes from a source such as a candle. They are less aware of this in the case of an object such as a book, when they think that vision has more to do with looking.

Many children do not understand that light is essential for vision, and are convinced that they can see in the dark. This is probably because they associate 'darkness' with being in bed at night, when there is in fact some light entering the room from the windows or under the door.

This made the answers to the question: Why can't you see in the dark? seem a little strange. Here are some of the responses:

I see shadows.
When the curtains are open I can see.
Because there's no light, you can see a little bit!
We ain't eating carrots.

Few children at Key Stage 2 are able to give the scientific explanation of vision, which is that we see objects because light is scattered off them and into our eyes.

Helping children to develop their ideas

The chart on the next page shows how you can help children to develop their ideas from starting points which have given rise to different ideas.

The centre rectangle contains a starter question.

The surrounding 'thought bubbles' contain the sorts of ideas expressed by children.

The further ring of rectangles contains questions posed by teachers in response to the ideas expressed by the children. These questions are meant to prompt children to think about their ideas.

The outer ovals indicate ways in which the children might respond to the teacher's questions.

Some of the shapes have been left blank, as a sign that other ideas may be encountered and other ways of helping children to develop their ideas may be tried.

1 Light sources and their representation

For work on light sources you will need powerful torches, a projector, white card and chalk.

a Identifying and grouping light sources

Children could look around the classroom and other places in the school to see what light sources they can discover.

Once the children have identified the light sources around them they could compile this information into a pictogram. The easiest way to do this is to ask the children to transfer their drawings of light sources on to separate small squares of paper, drawing one light source on each square of paper. Then ask them to decide how they could group their answers.

COMMUNICATING. INTERPRETING RESULTS AND FINDINGS

Some children may only list primary light sources; others may give a mixture.

LIGHT IS SCATTERED FROM MANY SURFACES, AND DOES NOT JUST COME FROM PRIMARY SOURCES

 Which were the most common light sources?
Which were the most unusual?

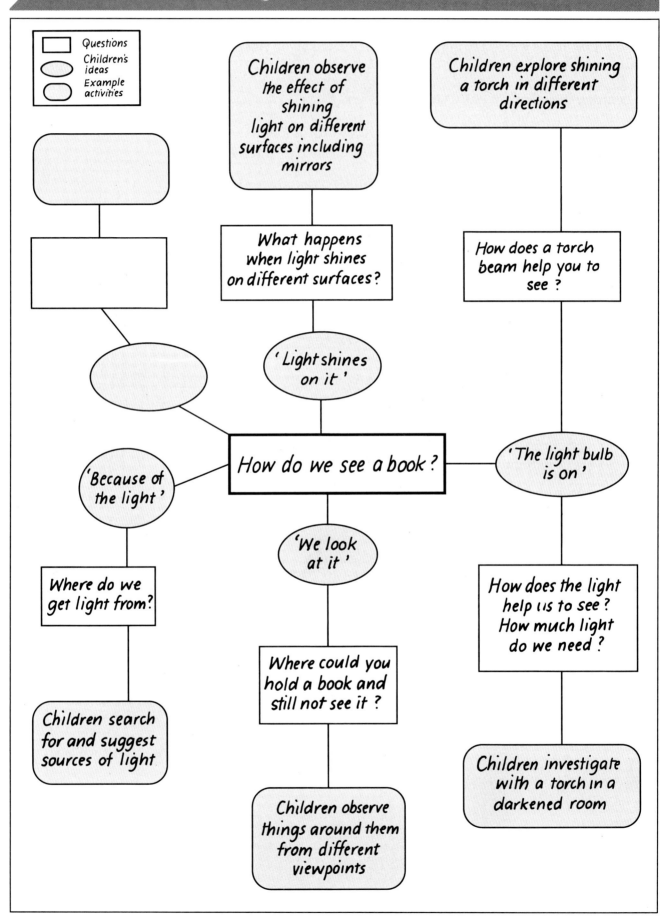

Questions
Children's ideas
Example activities

Children observe the effect of shining light on different surfaces including mirrors

Children explore shining a torch in different directions

What happens when light shines on different surfaces?

How does a torch beam help you to see?

'Light shines on it'

How do we see a book?

'The light bulb is on'

'Because of the light'

'We look at it'

Where do we get light from?

Where could you hold a book and still not see it?

How does the light help us to see? How much light do we need?

Children search for and suggest sources of light

Children observe things around them from different viewpoints

Children investigate with a torch in a darkened room

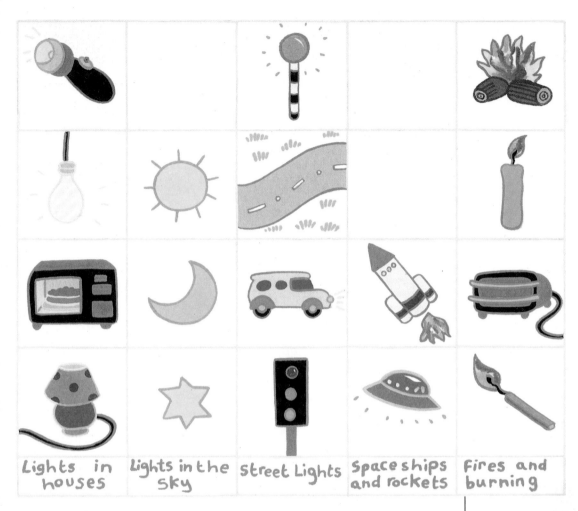

| Lights in houses | Lights in the Sky | Street Lights | Space ships and rockets | Fires and burning |

it

For this pictogram children chose their own categories and grouped sources of light, using a word processor.

Children classified light sources according to whether the light came from something burning or not.

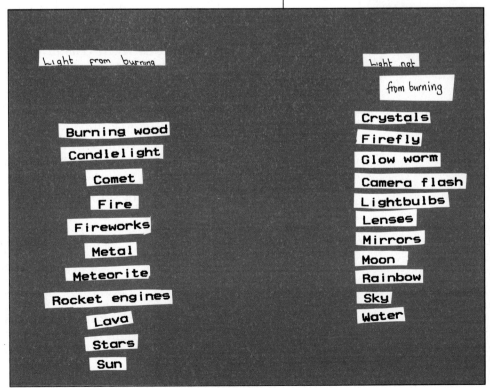

Light from burning

Burning wood
Candlelight
Comet
Fire
Fireworks
Metal
Meteorite
Rocket engines
Lava
Stars
Sun

Light not from burning

Crystals
Firefly
Glow worm
Camera flash
Lightbulbs
Lenses
Mirrors
Moon
Rainbow
Sky
Water

pb

Children could also think of light sources used in celebrations. *Light* gives some examples.

b Discussing the effectiveness of light sources

From the children's responses to the question above, much fruitful discussion may arise about the effectiveness of these light sources.

Questions to prompt widening of the discussion could include:

Q *Can the light from a lighthouse be seen during the day?*
Would a lighthouse be a good way of warning people of danger in towns and cities?
Why do lighthouses work well on the coast?
How do ships make use of the signals from lighthouses?
What happens if it is foggy?
How do motorists know which traffic signals they must look at?
What would happen if motorists could see all of the lights at the same time?

 **t**

IMPLICIT IN THE IDEA OF WARNINGS AND SIGNALS IS THAT LIGHT TRAVELS FROM A SOURCE TO A RECEIVER

Discussing these and other questions will raise many opportunities for further investigations, allowing children to investigate their ideas about warning lights, signals and light travelling.

More about light contains information about lighthouses and a story about signalling which could be used to give further ideas.

 pb

GENERAL

The children can test their ideas further by carrying out practical work with torches, light-bulbs, reflectors, and so on.

c How far does light travel?

e

The following activities can also be used to help children to develop their thinking about light sources and light travelling.

Ask the children to shine a torch against a wall or a screen (perhaps white card) in a dark place. Encourage them to think about how the light gets from the torch to the wall or screen.

Q *How do you think the light gets from the torch to the screen?*
Is the light at the torch, at the wall, in between?

The children may want to show that the light does exist between the torch and the screen by blocking the light with their hand or a piece of card.

Children could look around the classroom and other places in the school to discover any other sources of light. In doing this they may find light reflected from such secondary sources as walls, water, and cars.

The concept of light travelling in straight lines is very difficult for children to understand because they can see only the effects of this. One of the more obvious effects is that shadows are formed because light cannot travel round corners.

If you shine a torch on an object such as a wall, it is possible to see that the light has 'shone' from the torch to the wall because there is a patch of light. But this does not help to explain how the light travelled from the torch to the wall.

Asking children questions about an everyday event may help them to think of explanations.

Ask them to think about a projector:

Q *How could you show that the light goes from the projector to the screen?*

One way of doing this would be to hold a piece of card at various points between the light source and the screen to see if the light can be seen.

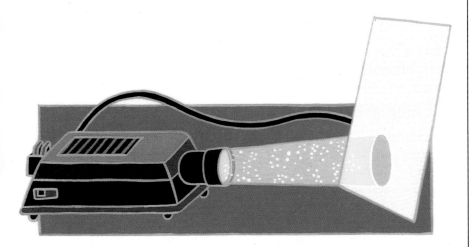

Another way is to use chalk dust to make the beam of light visible.

CHALK DUST MAY CAUSE ASTHMA

The children may have suggestions about how they could test their own ideas on the way light travels.

Children may be unaware of how we use beams of light in our daily lives. *More about light* provides information about the uses of light beams.

pb

d The representation of light

Children may be interested in exploring the ways in which lights of all kinds are illustrated in children's books and comics. They could also discover the ways in which artists represent light in paintings. This could be followed up by visiting an art gallery and looking at the way light has been shown in pictures throughout the ages. (Many art galleries are pleased to arrange a special talk around a chosen theme.)

The children could make a collection of pictures showing lights, from comics, paintings and photographs. This could lead to interesting discussions about the ideas the artists may have had about light.

The pictures in *More about light* could be used for discussion.

Ask the children to compare their own ideas and drawings with those they have discovered in other pictures.

AT 1 — COMMUNICATING

2 Vision

This work will have more meaning for children who have already carried out some investigations into reflections. However, seeing reflections involves vision and you have to start somewhere! Although they will not reach a full understanding of vision, they may partly understand some elements of the scientific explanation.

The children's own explanations of how they see will form a useful introduction to work about vision.

AT 1 — COMMUNICATING

a Comparing ideas

Use children's responses to the starter activities (page 34) as a starting point. This is a particularly fruitful opportunity for them to compare their ideas with those of the others. Have they all given the same explanation of how they see things? (This could be done in groups of two, or in larger groups.) What different explanations are given? Children might read out their explanations and compare them with those of their friends. Discovering others' ideas can often cause children to modify their own. Older children may also wish to compare their ideas with those of scientists.

b Seeing in the dark

 Can you explain why you can't see in the dark?

The children could write down their response before sharing it with others.

 Where could we take this book so that we would not see it?

At first the children are likely to suggest hiding the book.

Q *Can you be in a place where you could hold the book but still not see it?*

Going to a dark place, for example a dark storeroom, may help children to understand the need for light for vision.

 Q *What happens to colour in the dark?*

Get the children to watch the transition from dark to light as a door is slowly opened and closed in a darkened room with a light outside.

 Q *What can you see in this room?*

Ask a child to look around the room, and at the same time tell the others what she or he can see.

Now black out the room and gradually close the door. Ask the children what they can see now:

 Q *Can you see anything at all? If you can, what is helping you to see?*
Is there any light in the room?
Where is the light coming from?

Ask the children to write and make drawings about their experience of going to a dark place.

If it is not possible to black out the room, a large cardboard box painted black on the inside can be used instead. Coloured objects can be put in the box and viewed through a spyhole, with and without a lid on the box.

Discuss folklore and vocabulary associated with the dark.

There are many everyday expressions which confuse children in their ideas about vision. Children could discuss their own understanding of these. *More about light* has some examples.

Many children may think that carrots help them to see in the dark, or that they cannot see because they have not been eating carrots. This myth goes back to the Second World War, when

AT 1	OBSERVING

t	LIGHT IS ESSENTIAL FOR VISION – WE CANNOT SEE IN THE DARK BECAUSE OF THE ABSENCE OF LIGHT

AT 1	COMMUNICATING. INTERPRETING RESULTS AND FINDINGS

 e

 v

 pb

the British Ministry of Information deliberately started a rumour that pilots were fed carrots to improve their night vision. It was an attempt to stop the Germans from finding out that the British had developed radar sets small enough to carry on an aircraft. Carrots contain beta carotene, which the body turns to vitamin A. Deficiency of this vitamin can actually cause night blindness. But a surplus does not improve vision.

c How do other creatures see in the dark?

Ask children:

 What creatures can you think of which are more active at night?
Do you think that they are able to see in the dark?
If so, how do you think they are able to see in the dark?

The children should discuss their ideas before they investigate possible answers. They could refer to secondary sources, make a poster, or possibly visit a 'twilight world' at a zoo.

Light may help children to discuss animals which see in the dark.

d Finding out about reflected light and vision

It is difficult for children to understand that we can see because light is scattered from objects into our eyes. Many children (and adults) think that we see simply by looking and, although they may realize the need for light, they do not understand the actual connection between our eyes, the light source and an object.

The following activity may help children to gain some understanding of this difficult scientific idea.

Two children working together stand one behind the other. The one in front holds a mirror so that she can see the light from a torch held by the child behind.

COMMUNICATING

Ask the children to draw and write their explanation of how they see the light from the torch. This will help them to form their own ideas about the way we see objects, and may make them aware of light travelling to their eyes.

This may prompt children to ask further questions about how eyes work. Information about this can be found in *Light*. Sometimes what we see has more to do with perception than vision. Children could look at the optical illusion puzzles in *Light*.

e Making a pinhole camera

Making and using a pinhole camera is another activity which may help children towards an understanding of vision.

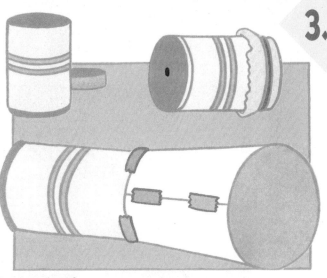

It is suitable for children who have done some previous work on light, which makes it more likely that they will understand how light can enter a small aperture and form an image on a screen.

Kits for making pinhole cameras are readily available. Alternatively, the children can make one by using a tin with a small hole in the base. (Make sure there are no sharp edges.) Greaseproof paper is stretched over the open end and secured with an elastic band. To use the camera, point the pinhole towards a bright source of light. The image will appear upside down on the greaseproof paper. It will work better if a roll of paper is wrapped round the open end to shield it from the surrounding light.

THE IMAGE IS FORMED BY LIGHT ENTERING THE CAMERA THROUGH THE PINHOLE; IT IS INVERTED

The children may be more concerned with the 'magical' effect than with the explanation of how light enters the camera to form the image. Ask them:

Q *How do you think the camera works?*

This question could form the basis of some interesting discussions. If you simply offer children the 'correct' explanation, they are unlikely to understand it. They may, however, raise some questions and expect answers. It is important only to offer the children as much information as they can understand at one time. The full explanation can be developed in stages. Chapter 5 'Background science' gives more information.

AT 1   COMMUNICATING

Children could look at the effects of light on paper and find out more about early photography. *Light* includes some ideas on this.

pb

The work on reflections and the nature of light should help children towards an understanding of vision. However, this is a difficult area for children in the primary school. The investigations they have carried out will provide them with a wide range of experiences which they can draw on at a later stage, when they are able to understand more of the scientific explanation of vision.

As an extension, children could investigate moving pictures and how they were developed from Victorian parlour games. *Light* could form a starting point.

pb

Reflections and shadows

AREAS FOR INVESTIGATION

◆ The reflection of light from various surfaces, and the formation of reflected images.

◆ Transparent, translucent and opaque materials.

◆ Shadows of children, and of objects.

KEY IDEAS

◆ Light travels through some materials but not through others.

◆ The position, shape, and size of a shadow depend upon the position of the object in relation to the position of the light source.

◆ Light is reflected off objects.

◆ *Light travels in straight lines.

(*Asterisks indicate ideas which will be developed more fully in later key stages.)

A LOOK AT
reflections and shadows

When light meets a surface some of the light is reflected. Some surfaces reflect light better than others, and an object appears bright when its surface reflects most of the light that falls on it. Smooth surfaces such as mirrors can produce clear images, which we refer to as 'reflections'.

Light does not pass through opaque materials. When light meets an opaque object a shadow is formed on the opposite side of the object to the light source. Normally some light reaches the area of the shadow by being reflected off other objects, so it appears dark rather than totally black.

Nearly all the light meeting a transparent material passes through it, and so we see through it clearly. Materials which allow only a little light to pass through them are described as translucent. Many plastic objects are translucent.

The direction in which a beam of light is travelling can be changed by reflection from a mirror; or by passing the beam through a transparent material such as glass or water.

Finding out children's ideas

STARTER ACTIVITIES

1 Reflections

Some of the following activities can be used to help children to develop their ideas on reflections.

a Making a collection

Ask the children to make a collection of objects: one set in which they can see their faces and another set in which they cannot see their faces.

b Drawing reflections

 What is a reflection?

Get the children to produce annotated drawings to explain their ideas.

Also ask them:

 Where have you seen your reflection?

c Discussion

Some children may use the word 'reflection' to talk about the images they see. Other children may not have come across the word before. You may feel that it is necessary to introduce some vocabulary work here to enable the children to talk about their ideas. They may need to use words such as 'reflection' and 'reflector'; alternatively, this could be left to a later stage when children have had more practical experience. If you do introduce these words, discussion can include questions such as the following:

Which things make good reflectors?
Why can you see your reflection in some things and not in others?
Why do shiny surfaces make better reflectors?
Do all the reflectors give true reflections?
How do some reflectors change your reflections?
Try to explain how you see your reflection in a mirror.

2 Shadows

a What is a shadow?

Ask the children to write down what they think a shadow is. They could discuss their answers with a friend or with a group of children. Perhaps they could compile a class list of their suggestions.

b Finding out about the position of shadows

Get the children to make a paper shadow by drawing round a member of the class (preferably one of the smaller children) lying on a large piece of dark sugar paper, and then cutting out the shape. Ask the 'template' child to stand in an open space in the classroom. Are the other children able to predict where the shadow will be if the Sun is shining behind him or her? Ask individual children if they can place the template to show where the shadow would be. (A yellow paper circle can be used to represent the Sun.)

Q *Where would your shadow be if the Sun were shining behind you?*

Ask the children to draw a picture to show where their shadow would be in this case. You could try both this activity and the practical exercise to see if they choose the same position for the shadow in both cases.

Q *Can you think of some good places to find shadows?*

At this point you could ask the children to devise their own investigations to find out more about shadows.

Children's ideas

1 Ideas about reflections

Children may not have come across the word 'reflection' before. Even if they have, they may confuse 'reflection' with 'shadow' and use the two words interchangeably. Children are likely to be less familiar with the idea of reflections than with shadows. By exploring both shadows and reflections children will widen their experience and understand more of the two phenomena and the differences between them.

The following examples illustrate some of the ideas which children have about reflections. The first two show the common confusion between shadows and reflections.

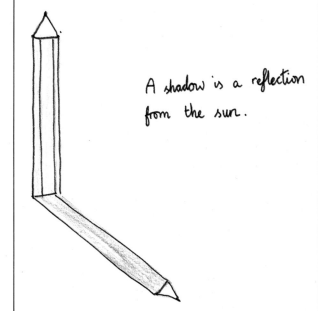

A shadow is a reflection from the sun.

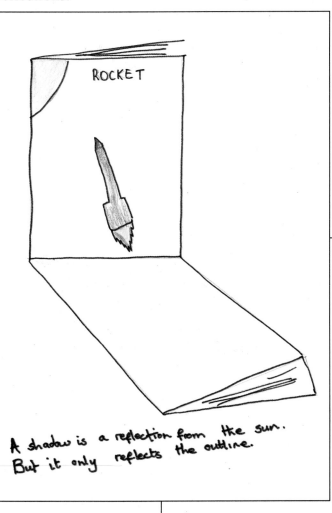

A shadow is a reflection from the sun. But it only reflects the outline.

A reflection is like a photograph that moves. It is like when you look in the mirror, water or your shadow. You can see what you are doing in a reflection.

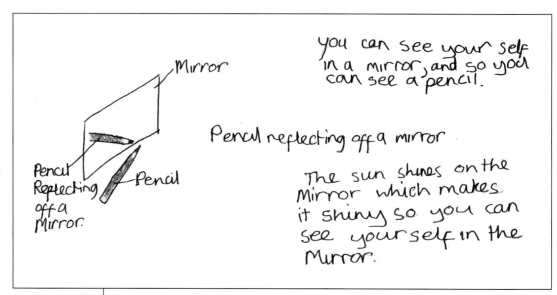

Mirror

Pencil
Reflecting
off a
Mirror.

Pencil

you can see your self in a mirror, and so you can see a pencil.

Pencil reflecting off a mirror.

The sun shines on the Mirror which makes it shiny so you can see yourself in the Mirror.

When the spoon shines you look at it and you will see a reflection of you.

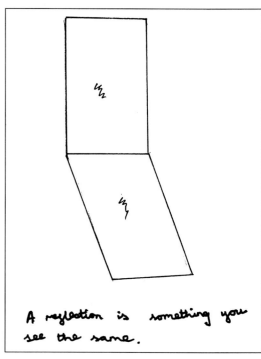

A reflection is something you see the same.

When the light (sun) is shining on a kettle you can see your self clearly.

The following were typical responses to the question: 'What is a reflection?'

> *A reflection comes from a mirror.*
> *When you look in the mirror, there's another you.*
> *The car's got reflections in it.*
> *I don't know what a reflection is!*

The children who drew the pictures in this section are aware of some of the reflections they often see in shiny surfaces. They have not yet understood how light from an object is reflected from the surface.

> *A reflection is when a beam of light is bouncing off shiny things or when you see yourself.*
> *Light rebounding and hitting something solid.*
> *A reflection is when you beam a light on a mirror, it reflects back off on to you.*
> *A reflection is yourself looking back at you in a mirror or a piece of glass.*

Children may already be able to explain reflections in terms of light bouncing off a shiny surface, and no longer confuse them with shadows. These examples show that some children have a fairly sophisticated view of what a reflection is and correctly associate it with 'bouncing', and with shiny surfaces and mirrors. Few children at this stage can give anything like the scientific explanation; this requires an understanding of how light striking a flat surface at a certain angle is reflected from it at an equal angle, rather than being diffused in all directions as it would be by a rough surface.

2 Ideas about shadows

The exploratory activities will have revealed some of the ideas your children have about shadows. The children's pictures and your discussions about them may tell you:

◆ whether they know what a shadow is;
◆ whether they think shadows are grey, black or coloured.

The following examples were typical of the responses given to 'What is a shadow?'

> *You! When you look down it's black, not colourful.*
> *It looks like me.*
> *It's the black thing that always follows you when it's sunny!*

> It's dark, it's the same size as a book or whatever else it is, but you can't see the colours.
>
> A shadow is something when the Sun's light beams down on us. Because we are opaque the light does not go through us, it causes the light to bounce off us which means that the rest of the light goes past.

You may also discover:

◆ whether the children understand that a bright light is needed for a shadow to be formed;

◆ whether they understand that light will go through some materials but not others (they will not necessarily associate this with the formation of shadows);

◆ whether they think that shadows are attached to objects (shadows can be attached or detached depending on where the source of light is coming from);

◆ whether they think that shadows are upside down or the same way up as objects (they can be either, depending on where the light source and the observer are in relation to the object);

◆ whether they confuse shadows and reflections.

Some children think that a shadow is the same thing as a reflection. They often use the words 'shadow' and 'reflection' interchangeably and appear to think that shadows and reflections are the same thing:

> A shadow is a reflection of you. A shadow comes out when it is sunny because the Sun gives a beam of light.

A few children are able to give a sophisticated definition of a shadow, showing that they have a good understanding of what shadows are and how they are formed:

> A shadow is just light rays beaming down and hitting something. The object will not let the Sun's rays past and it makes a shadow.

The drawings on the left were produced when children were asked to draw a picture to show where their shadow would be if the Sun were shining behind them.

These children appeared to think that a shadow 'surrounds' a person. One child drew the shadow as a very simple outline. A possible alternative explanation for these drawings is that the children thought that a shadow always appears behind a person, and that in trying to show this they have drawn it so that it appears that the shadow is surrounding the person.

Talking to the children about their pictures will clarify their ideas.

Pictures often show the same surface detail on the shadow as there is on the person – for example, faces and clothes. The children who drew these pictures have not yet observed that they cannot see such detail on shadows.

The pictures opposite show the shadows drawn in the correct position, but still with details of faces and clothes on the shadows.

The children who drew these pictures were clear about the relative position of the Sun and the shadow. They drew the shadow as a dark patch on the ground, similar in shape to the outline of the body.

Helping children to develop their ideas

The chart on the next page shows how you can help children to develop their ideas.

The centre rectangles contain starter questions.

The surrounding 'thought bubbles' contain the sorts of ideas expressed by children.

The further ring of rectangles contains questions posed by teachers in response to the ideas expressed by the children. These questions are meant to prompt children to think about their ideas.

The outer ovals indicate ways in which the children might respond to the teacher's questions.

Some of the shapes have been left blank, as a sign that other ideas may be encountered and other ways of helping children to develop their ideas may be tried.

Reflections and shadows

Further exploration with both shadows and reflections will help children to give more accurate explanations of the two. Children will also benefit from specific vocabulary work which helps them to sort out the differences in meaning between 'shadow' and 'reflection'.

1 Reflections

a Shining a light at different surfaces

Children could extend their ideas about reflections by shining a light on a collection of objects, some dull, some shiny; these could be the objects already used in 'Making a collection' (page 52).

Q *What do you notice happening when you shine a light on*
◆ *a collection of shiny objects?*
◆ *a collection of dull objects?*

Get the children to carry out investigations with different kinds of lights and different surfaces, such as paper, card and fabric of various types and colours. The children could try shining a torch on different surfaces. If possible, do this in a darkened room.

Q *On which surfaces can you see the light best?*
How far away can you stand and still see the light?
How do you think you could test this?

WE SEE OBJECTS BECAUSE LIGHT TRAVELS FROM THEM TO OUR EYES; SHINY AND DULL OBJECTS REFLECT LIGHT IN DIFFERENT WAYS

AT 1 — OBSERVING

Helping children to develop their ideas about reflections and shadows

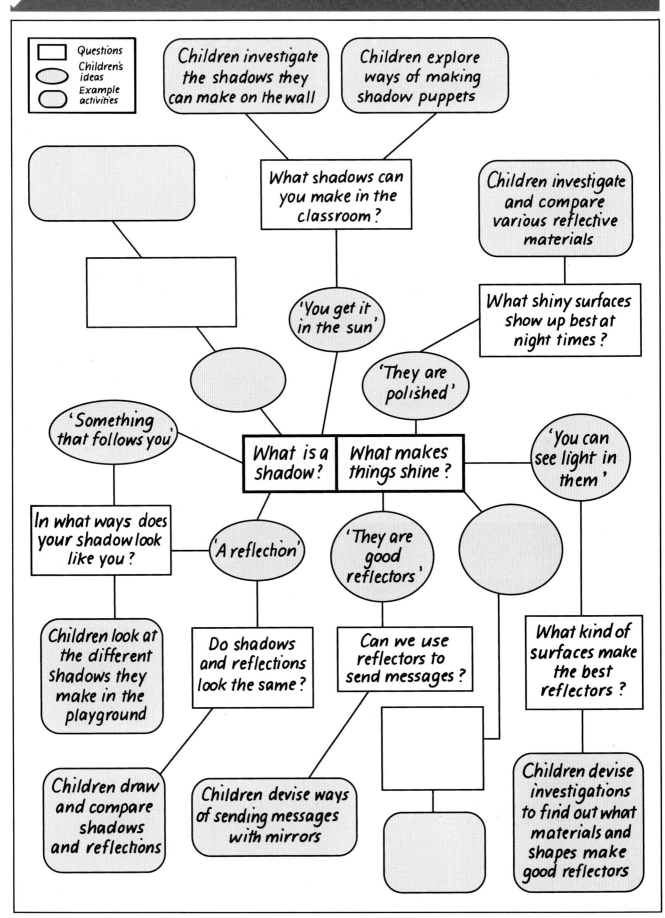

Questions

Children's ideas

Example activities

Children investigate the shadows they can make on the wall

Children explore ways of making shadow puppets

What shadows can you make in the classroom?

Children investigate and compare various reflective materials

What shiny surfaces show up best at night times?

'You get it in the sun'

'They are polished'

'Something that follows you'

What is a shadow?

What makes things shine?

'You can see light in them'

In what ways does your shadow look like you?

'A reflection'

'They are good reflectors'

Children look at the different shadows they make in the playground

Do shadows and reflections look the same?

Can we use reflectors to send messages?

What kind of surfaces make the best reflectors?

Children draw and compare shadows and reflections

Children devise ways of sending messages with mirrors

Children devise investigations to find out what materials and shapes make good reflectors

b Using mirrors and reflectors

Many investigations can be devised around mirrors and reflectors. (Use plastic mirrors if possible, or put tape across the back and round sharp edges.)

A useful way of helping children to extend their ideas about reflections is to give the children small mirrors so that they can see their reflections in them. Ask the children for their explanations of how they see their reflections.

AT 1   GENERAL

You could also get the children to use the mirror to reflect light from the Sun, a torch or a light-bulb against a wall.

The investigations which follow will help children to clarify their ideas further.

! IT IS DANGEROUS TO REFLECT SUNLIGHT INTO PEOPLE'S EYES

c Examining a torch

Children could examine a torch to see what it consists of, and then draw and label the parts.

Q *What helps to make the light appear 'bigger'?*
What do you think reflectors do?
What are reflectors made of?

d Which materials and shapes make the best reflectors?

The children could devise an investigation to find out which materials make the best reflectors – for example, silver and gold foil and card; white and coloured, shiny and matt paper and card; fabrics; wood.

Ask them to make a list of the materials they would like to try out.

You can also ask:

Q *Which shapes make the best reflectors?*

Let them try various shapes to find out which make good reflectors. If necessary you could suggest some, such as a large flat circle, a cone, and a box.

e Seeing behind you

 How could you use a mirror to see behind you?

Ask the children to try this.

They may suggest various devices – perhaps a mirror on a stick, or something more complicated such as a periscope.

Light gives examples of how mirrors are used in everyday life.

f Sending messages round corners with mirrors

As well as helping children to understand more about how mirrors can be used as reflectors, this activity may help children towards an understanding about light travelling in straight lines.

They could carry out the following investigation in groups of up to four children.

 Try to think of a way of sending a 'light message' round a corner from one friend to another.

One way of doing this is for children to work together. One holds a torch, another holds a mirror, and a third holds a piece of white card for a screen. (Use plastic mirrors if possible, or put tape across the back and round sharp edges.)

Ask the children to draw a picture to explain what happens during their investigations. They can use their drawings to talk about their ideas in more detail, or they can annotate them, writing down their explanation.

Children could develop the idea of sending messages with mirrors and lights. They could try different numbers of mirrors, different strengths of light, and sending a message round more than one corner or round other obstacles such as a screen.

Another variation of this activity is to get the children, in groups of four, to work out how they can send a light beam all the way round a table. For this, they will need a torch and three mirrors. It may help if they anchor the mirrors in position with Plasticine or Blu-Tack.

Ask the children to explain how they think it is possible for the light message to be sent round the table in this way. They could explain their ideas in an annotated drawing. This could be used as the basis of a group discussion so that children can share their ideas. Alternatively, get each group of children to work out an explanation between them, so that they share their ideas as they work out the explanation.

A harder question is:

 How can light from the window (not the direct light from the Sun) be used for sending messages across the room?

g Mountain rescue

Get the children to think how mirrors could be used as part of safety equipment carried by mountain walkers and explorers.

 How could you use a mirror if you were in trouble on a mountain?
How could it help in getting you rescued?

Ask the children to draw and write about their ideas.

More about light features a story which looks at this.

h Reflectors and safety

You can let the children look at a bicycle to find out about the various safety devices to do with lights. The bicycle should have lights and, if possible, white front and amber wheel-mounted reflectors as well as the standard red rear one.

More about light includes information about cycling and safety.

These questions could be used to suggest lines of investigation.

 How do the safety devices work?
Which of these are reflectors?
Are all the reflectors the same?
Do you think they would work better when a car's headlights are shining on them? How could you test this?
Is there anything on the bike which actually gives out light?

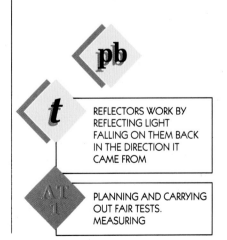

LIGHT
COLOURS
REFLECT MORE
LIGHT THAN
DARK ONES,
FLUORESCENT
COLOURS
EVEN MORE

GENERAL

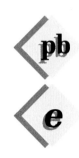

The children could also find out about the colours which reflect the most light. (See also 'Road safety', page 84.)

i Further investigations using mirrors: symmetry

There are many investigations which children could carry out to explore symmetry, so the following list is only a summary:

- looking at the symmetry of letters;
- mirror writing;
- investigating the symmetry of shapes;
- looking for symmetry in traditional patterns such as in Islamic, Rangoli, Fair Isle, Greek and Roman art;
- making patterns using two or more mirrors;
- looking at reflections in more than one mirror;
- investigating what happens when the angle between the mirrors is altered;
- making a simple kaleidoscope (see below);
- using a computer program to produce patterns – children can investigate these for symmetry.

Light and *More about light* suggest further activities on reflection.

For most of these you will need mirrors, and for some small counters or cubes.

j Making a kaleidoscope

Either you or the children should stick three small rectangular mirrors together with the reflecting side inside, using sticky tape. (Use plastic mirrors if possible.) Cover one end with white tissue or greaseproof paper. Cut some very small pieces of coloured acetate and put them inside. Cover the other end with cling film. The children should hold the kaleidoscope up to the light and slowly turn it.

Q *Can you explain how your kaleidoscope works?*

k Pictures of reflections

Give the children some pictures of reflections to look at, or let them look for pictures of reflections in books. There are some in *Light* and *More about light*.

What kind of surfaces do the reflections appear in?

Do the reflections look exactly the same as the objects?

Let the children make their own pictures of reflections.

If there is an area of open water near the school, take the children to look at the reflections on a bright, clear day. To help them to observe carefully, they could draw a picture to show the reflections.

BE CAREFUL WITH CHILDREN NEXT TO OPEN WATER

Once the children have explored both shadows and reflections, it may be useful to ask them to think of similarities and differences between shadows and reflections. This will give you some idea of the understanding they have arrived at.

The children could make a chart to compare their ideas about shadows and reflections.

l Light travelling through different materials

The aim here is to enable children to make predictions and to carry out explorations, but not necessarily to reach a scientific understanding of how light behaves when it travels through different media.

You will need prisms, a tank of water, lenses and torches.

Ideas about refraction (bending) of light do not need to be mentioned here. The children could simply predict what they think will happen and then make their observations.

Q *What do you think will happen when you shine a light through water/lenses/a prism?*
Will the light go through it?
Is the light the same, brighter or not so bright at the other side?
What do you notice when you shine the light through it?
What happens to the light when it goes through it?
Which other materials can you find which light can travel through?

OBSERVING. PREDICTING

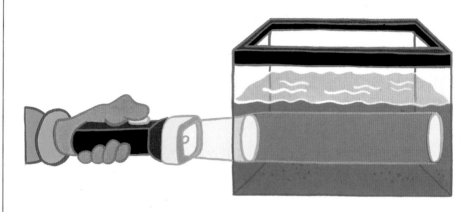

The children could make a list of things which they think a light will shine through. Then they can test their ideas to find out if they are right. Try this with various plastic objects, bottles, a window, and so on.

This investigation may provide an opportunity to introduce the words 'transparent', 'translucent' and 'opaque'.

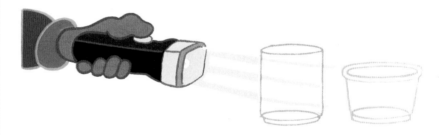

After the children have tested the materials, ask:

Q *Were your ideas right?*
Why do you think that the light will shine through these things?

2 Shadows

a General exploration

You will need powerful torches and a large variety of materials including card, fabrics, leather, and plastic, coloured paper, and a large sheet of white card, paper or fabric for a screen. Provide some plastic geometric shapes, or cut these out of card. Also provide some familiar objects with interesting shapes.

Give the children these things and let them devise ways of testing their own ideas about shadows. The starter activities will have aroused their interest and given them ideas for investigations. Exploring in an unstructured way can lead to discoveries which the children may not come across otherwise. Also, you will find that children enjoy making their own discoveries!

b Representing shadows in drawings

Give the children copies of one of the copiable sheets on pages 31 or 32 and ask them to draw the shadows on the picture. The pictures are of a room at night and a room during the day.

A simpler alternative is for children to draw the shadow of a single object, such as a tree on a sunny day.

The children's pictures will show how they represent shadows, whether they are able to recognize what they are, and what they understand of the relationship between an object, its shadow and the light source. The pictures will form a useful insight into children's thinking and can be used as the basis of a discussion which could help them to develop their thinking further.

The poem 'Shadow race' in *Light* could also be used for discussion.

c Which materials can light go through?

Give the children a wide range of materials so that they can see if light will pass through them. They will need to think carefully about how they can devise a test. Are they simply going to put the material over the end of the torch, or can they think of a better way of carrying out a fair test?

LIGHT CAN TRAVEL THROUGH SOME MATERIALS BUT NOT THROUGH OTHERS

You will need torches; mirrors; plastic geometric shapes, assorted materials, a card, paper or fabric screen; and a shadow box – a cardboard box with a hole at one end and the other end replaced with a piece of white paper. The children can put the material to be tested over the hole to see if the torchlight shines on the screen.

Ask the children to predict which materials will let light through before they start the test.

PREDICTING. PLANNING AND CARRYING OUT FAIR TESTS

d Looking at our shadows

Ask the children to draw pictures of what they think their shadow might look like. Then they can investigate their ideas by looking at actual shadows. The best place to carry out this work is in the playground on a bright sunny day.

OBSERVING

There will be many lines of investigation, which could be

3.2

 SHADOWS CANNOT USUALLY BE SEEN WHEN THERE IS NO DIRECT LIGHT

prompted by asking some of these questions:

Q *Where is your shadow?*
Does it look just like you?
How is it different from you?
Does your shadow always stay in the same position?
Can you change the shape of your shadow?
Can you stand in a place where you can't see your shadow?

! WARN CHILDREN NOT TO LOOK DIRECTLY AT THE SUN

e The position of shadows

This activity lets children explore the relationship between the Sun (or other light source) and their shadow.

Q *Can you point to where your shadow is with one hand and to the Sun with the other hand?*

Ask the children to face in a different direction and then repeat the exercise.

 Do you notice anything about where your arms are pointing?

Encourage them to move about and try the experiment several times. See whether they notice that there is a pattern in the way their arms point – always in opposite directions. It is important that you do not introduce this 'rule' to the children, but that you leave them to discover it for themselves.

A useful way of recording shadows is to take photographs. It is sometimes easier to see what your own shadow looks like from a photograph. Children could have fun with this by taking pictures of their shadow going across different surfaces, for example partly on the playground and partly on a wall. They could also compare pictures of their shadows taken at different times of the day.

There are examples of shadows in photographs in *Time and Space*.

 Can you stand in a place where you can't see your shadow?

Are the children able to explain why they are not able to see their shadow in the places they have chosen?

A SHADOW IS ON THE OPPOSITE SIDE OF AN OBJECT TO THE LIGHT SOURCE – THE OBJECT, SHADOW AND LIGHT SOURCE ARE IN LINE WITH EACH OTHER

INTERPRETING RESULTS AND FINDINGS

INTERPRETING RESULTS AND FINDINGS

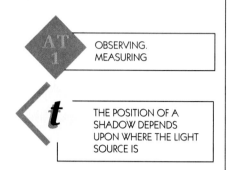

OBSERVING.
MEASURING

 Can you escape from your shadow?

The children may jump off the ground, or run to the shade.

Ask the children working in pairs to draw round one another's shadow in the playground. Later on the same day, bring them back to look at their shadow again. Is it the same?

 Is your shadow always in the same place? If not, why not?

Children could look at their shadows several times in the day, observing both the position and the size.

To avoid confusion, get the children to mark their shadow shapes with their names, and to draw round their feet so that they can stand in exactly the same place each time. (See also *The Earth in Space* teachers' guide.)

t THE POSITION OF A SHADOW DEPENDS UPON WHERE THE LIGHT SOURCE IS

f Silhouettes

Silhouettes are a useful way of looking at shadows inside the classroom, particularly in the winter months. They are also useful for following up the work in the playground, and especially for observing the effect of the distance between the object and the light source.

To make a silhouette, get one of the children to sit between a projector and the wall so that his or her shadow falls on to a large sheet of paper pinned to the wall.

Ask the children:

 How can you sit to make the most interesting shadow?
How far from the screen should you sit to make your shadow life-size?
What would you need to do to make your shadow larger/smaller?

Someone draws round the shadow on the paper. This silhouette can then be painted black or transferred to black paper before being cut out.

You could show the children the Victorian silhouette given opposite.

g Shadows of objects

The children could explore the school, indoors and out, looking for shadows. At first they may not realize that objects as well as people have shadows.

OBSERVING

Give the children a range of shapes and objects so that they can explore the shadows of familiar objects. You could try using

three-dimensional as well as two-dimensional shapes, but start with flat ones. (However, shadows of children are shadows of three-dimensional objects!)

The children could investigate:

- the size of shadows;
- their shape;
- their colour.

 How can any of these be changed?

Let them devise their own investigations to test their ideas.

Once they have started to explore their ideas, they could discuss how to devise a fair test.

AT 1   GENERAL

What will affect the shape of the shadow?
Are shadows always the same size as the object that makes them?
Is it possible to alter the size of shadows?
Is it possible to alter the colour of shadows?

The children can look at the effect of placing the object at different distances from the light source.

 What happens when the object is moved nearer/further away?

h Coloured shadows

Let the children experiment with different coloured backgrounds, coloured lights (these can be produced by using coloured acetate, or cellophane sweet wrappers), and different coloured objects. Powerful torches, a screen and a shadow box (see page 69) will also be needed.

Give the children a chance to predict the effect before they carry out each test.

Many of the possibilities can be discussed with the children beforehand so that they can try out their own suggestions.

i Shadow puppets

Much of the work about shadows could be incorporated into a project about shadow puppets.

 Light gives examples of different types of shadow puppets.

Before children make their shadow puppets, encourage them to think about some of the following:

 How do you make shadows?
What will you use for the light and the screen?

What will you make the puppets of?
Can you make puppets which give coloured shadows?
Can you show any details such as faces or clothes?
How will you hold and move the puppets?
If you want the shadows to look the same size as the
puppets, where will you need to hold them?

Many other questions will probably arise as the children try
out their ideas.

Suggestions for making shadow puppets

There are many ways for children to make their own shadow
puppets. One of the simplest is for children to cut out paper
shapes which they can put on an overhead projector. As the
children tell a story, they can push the puppets around on the
surface.

Proper Indonesian shadow puppets are held from below
behind a translucent screen, and lit from behind. Puppets of
this kind can be cut from fairly stiff card. Joints can be made by
using paper fasteners. The best way for children to operate
these is to stick Velcro to the back of the puppets and to the
ends of dowel rod. The dowel rods can then easily be
transferred to other puppets.

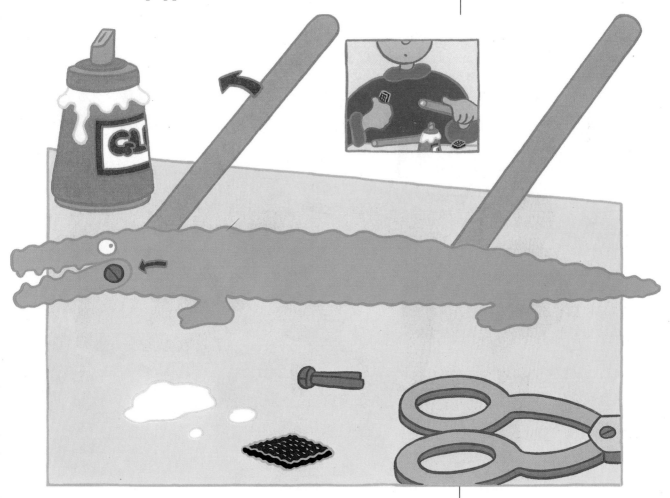

More sophisticated, coloured puppets can be made from card
in a similar way. 'Windows' can be cut in the card (not too big,

or the puppet will flop) and covered with coloured cellophane from sweet wrappers, or paper coloured with felt-tipped markers and made translucent by patting a little cooking oil into it after it is stuck on. Jointed limbs or other small parts can be cut from coloured acetate. Details can be drawn on the coloured parts with black felt-tipped marker.

It is important that the children have done some prior investigations into opaque, transparent and translucent materials so that they understand that puppets made in this way are translucent and allow some of the light to shine through. A red 'window' lets only red light through; other colours are stopped.

j Light sources and shadows

Older children could try the following activity, which may help them to realize that shadows are formed because light travels in straight lines.

Put a strong light in the middle of a darkened room – for example, a table lamp without a shade. Ask the children to stand in a circle round the lamp.

Get the children to make a shadow against the wall with their hands, and to look at the shadows which have been made by the other children. Then ask the children to draw and write an explanation of what happens. The children could discuss their ideas with each other.

 Q *Can you explain why everyone can make a shadow by using one light?*
If we put the light in a different place, do you think everyone could still make a shadow?

Try moving the light, or get the children to sit in different positions.

By doing this, children may gain some understanding of the idea that light radiates in all directions from a light source.

t | LIGHT TRAVELS FROM A LIGHT SOURCE UNTIL IT MEETS SOMETHING OPAQUE

AT 1 | PREDICTING. OBSERVING

Colour

AREAS FOR INVESTIGATION

- Colour in the natural environment.
- Colour in the built environment.
- The significance of colour in our daily lives.
- The effects produced by mixing paint, looking through coloured filters, and using coloured spinners.

KEY IDEAS

- Colours in the environment often have a particular significance for plants and animals, including humans – for example, warning coloration and camouflage.
- Different colours can be created by mixing coloured paints, or by using filters.

A LOOK AT
colour

White light can be split up into a range of colours, usually listed as red, orange, yellow, green, blue, indigo and violet. This range is known as the spectrum of white light, and can be seen in a rainbow.

A white surface reflects all colours of light. Other surfaces reflect certain colours; for example, red surfaces reflect only red light.

Because white surfaces are highly reflective they appear brighter than other surfaces. In general, any surface that appears brightly coloured is reflecting plenty of light and will tend to show up in faint light.

Mixing coloured lights gives other colours, an effect that is seen from a rotating 'colour spinner'. White light can be produced from three coloured lights: red, blue and green. These three colours are known as the primary colours in light, or the additive primary colours, because they create other colours by being added to each other. They cannot be mixed to make black.

In painting there are different primary colours: red, blue and yellow. Other colours can be made by mixing these coloured paints. These are known as the subtractive primary colours, because mixing them reduces the amount of light that the mixture reflects. They can be mixed to make black, but not white.

A colour filter allows only its own colour of light to pass through it. For example, only red light passes through a red filter. If two (or more) different-coloured filters are put over each other, only the colours which can go through both (or all) the filters will get through. This is a subtractive mixing process, and can produce black – that is, no light getting through.

• •

Note

Much of the work about colour at Key Stage 2 will have an emphasis on Sc1 rather than Sc4 due to the difficulty of developing some of the concepts associated with colour at this level. One of the areas of most difficulty is that of mixing colours.

While the scientific understanding of colour is best left to a later stage it is possible for children at Key Stage 2 to carry out interesting and exciting scientific investigations which

will increase their range of experiences and allow them to explore some of the effects they will encounter in their everyday lives. Much of the work will involve hypothesising, testing, observing, drawing conclusions, and recording and communicating ideas.

If properly handled, the work tackled at Key Stages 2 will form a useful foundation which can be built on later.

• •

Finding out children's ideas
■ STARTER ACTIVITIES

1 Colour in the environment

Children can make comparisons between colours found in different places. This may involve making comparisons between the range of colours found in the built environment and those found in the natural environment.

Another possibility is to compare different natural habitats and the types of living things found there, looking particularly at colour. Children could look at the colours of 'minibeasts' and their possible significance, or at the colours of flowering plants to see if these differ according to their location.

Alternatively, as a long-term project, children could carry out a study of one habitat throughout a year, investigating the way the colours change at different times of the year. (This work is linked with work in *The variety of life* teachers' guide and in *Living things in their environment* teachers' guide.)

Ask them first:

 Which colours do you think we will find in the school grounds/this habitat/this flowerbed (etc.)?
Which do you think will be the most common colours?
How do you think we could find out which are the most common colours?

2 Colour hunt

One way of finding out which colours are most common is to distribute pieces of coloured thread over a restricted area of ground. (You could hang them over flowers and shrubs as well as leaving them on the ground.) Distribute the same number of each colour of thread.

SOME CHILDREN, USUALLY BOYS, MAY BE COLOUR-BLIND

Send the children on a 'colour hunt', telling them to bring back only one thread at a time. As the threads are brought in, clip them to a long board or ruler in groups of five, in the order in which the children bring them to you.

 Which colours were found first?
Which took the longest to find?
What does that tell us about those colours?
Does this help you to think why some creatures are more difficult to see than others?
Why might it be an advantage for some animals to be more difficult to see than others?
What animals can you think of which are easy to see?
Why is it an advantage for some creatures to be brightly coloured?
Can you think of other ways to test your ideas about which colours are easy to see?

This work could lead the children into investigations of warning colours and camouflage.

Children's ideas

Many children are aware of the dominant colours in the natural and built environment, but are often less clear about the significance of some of these colours in our lives.

The colours make the country bright and pretty so that all the animals and people can inJoy. themself.

The children who drew these pictures thought in terms of things needing to look 'nice and bright', rather than of any scientific reasons for colour in the natural environment.

Children can often recall the colours of things such as buildings, signs and signals, or uniforms, but may not have thought of reasons for the choice of certain colours. However, they realize that we use colour to recognize certain people, cars, shops, and so on.

Children may not always use true colours to portray people, objects and scenes in their pictures, but choose the ones they find attractive.

Very few children appear to relate the colours of buildings to the materials they are made of.

Children are aware that bright colours are deliberately used because they stand out more clearly.

Most children are aware of different colours being used for warning lights and signals.

The lolli-pop lady helps the children cross the other side of the Road. The lolli-pop lady wears bright clothes so that everyone sees that she a lolli-pop lady.

Refuse collector's lorry yellow, so you would know it's not an odenary lorry.

The Larder shop. you can see the food inside. The canopy is so rain doint go on the window.

THE LARDER SHOP.

corting car

198

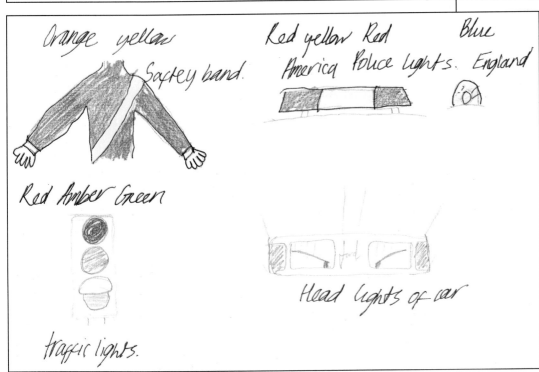

Orange yellow

Saftey band.

Red Amber Green

traffic lights.

Red yellow Red   Blue
America Police Lights. England

Head lights of car

Helping children to develop their ideas

The chart opposite shows how you can help children to develop their ideas.

The centre rectangle contains a starter question.

The surrounding 'thought bubbles' contain the sorts of ideas expressed by children.

The further ring of rectangles contains questions posed by teachers in response to the ideas expressed by the children. These questions are meant to prompt children to think about their ideas.

The outer ovals indicate ways in which the children might respond to the teacher's questions.

Some of the shapes have been left blank, as a sign that other ideas may be encountered and other ways of helping children to develop their ideas may be tried.

Colour in our daily lives

The following activities can be used to help children understand some of the uses of colours in our daily lives.

 How do people use the idea that some colours are easy to see and others more difficult?

Road safety, warning, and camouflage are some possible suggestions.

1 Road safety

Children could devise their own investigations into this subject. For instance, they could test their ideas about which colours show up more clearly.

Ask them:

AT 1	GENERAL

 Which colours do lollipop men and women usually wear?
How could you find out if these are the colours which help them to be seen most easily?
Think of a test to show if you are right.
Design a sign which will warn motorists about children crossing the road.
How would you find out how well the sign would work in the day?
Would the same sign also work well at night?
Would it show up well in the light from car headlights?
How could you test your ideas?
Which colours show more clearly in the dark?

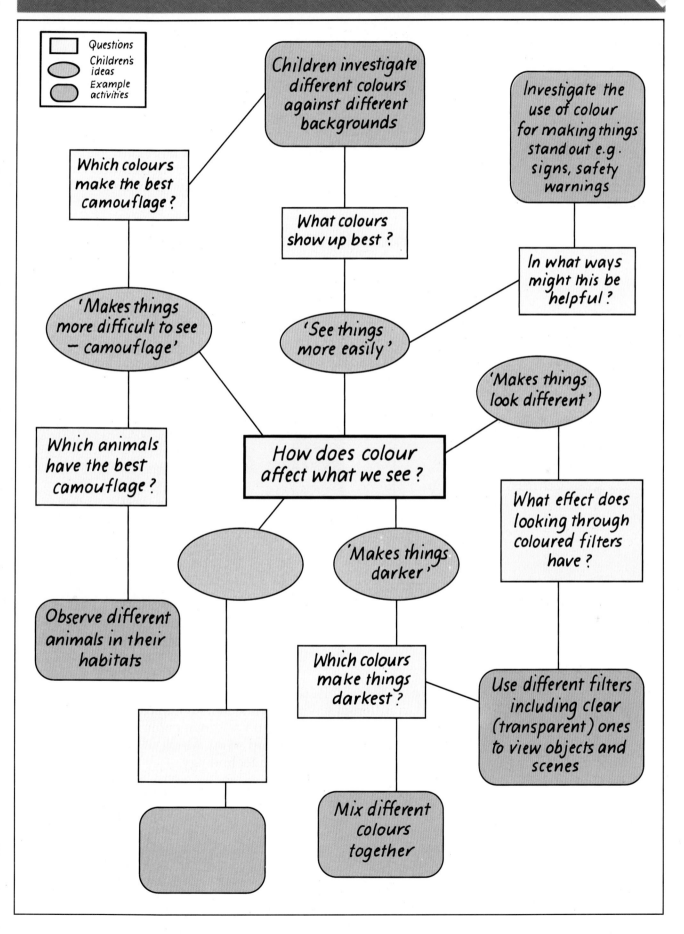

Key
- Questions
- Children's ideas
- Example activities

Children investigate different colours against different backgrounds

Which colours make the best camouflage?

Investigate the use of colour for making things stand out e.g. signs, safety warnings

What colours show up best?

In what ways might this be helpful?

'Makes things more difficult to see – camouflage'

'See things more easily'

'Makes things look different'

Which animals have the best camouflage?

How does colour affect what we see?

What effect does looking through coloured filters have?

'Makes things darker'

Observe different animals in their habitats

Which colours make things darkest?

Use different filters including clear (transparent) ones to view objects and scenes

Mix different colours together

BRIGHT COLOURS REFLECT
MOST OF THE LIGHT
THAT FALLS ON THEM

Children could try shining different coloured lights on different coloured objects to find out the effect. The story in *More about light* shows how coloured light affects the way we see things.

Children could devise investigations to find out which colours are more easily visible at night and during the day. This will help them towards an understanding of the significance of these colours in our lives.

They could use, for example, an assortment of coloured paper and fabric, a 'dark box' (this could be a large cardboard box, possibly painted black inside), and a torch. Children could discuss their own ideas about how to see into the box.

2 Colour in the environment

Another way of exploring colour in the environment is to ask the children to make a colour strip which they can then match with objects they find around them. After they have used the strip, ask:

Q *Are there any colours on the colour strip which you could not find in the classroom/outside?*

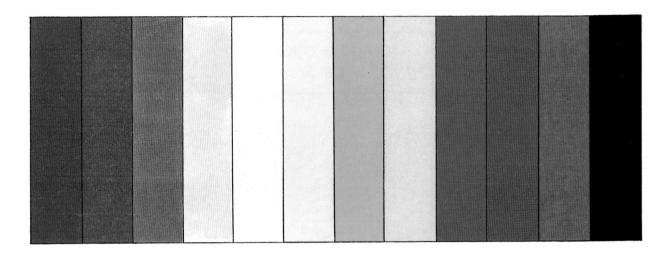

Encourage the children to think about the range of colours they find in different environments, and some possible reasons for it. Children could talk about their own colour preferences in clothes, food, decoration and so on. Much of this work could be linked to design work in technology.

The children could use the colour wheel in *Light* for these activities.

The children could explore a built area and a natural area, making their own pictures to record the dominant colours. They could then display the pictures to compare the main colours and the way they have represented them.

More simply, children could carry out a survey into the colours of front doors in a street near their school. The pictures below show the results of one group of children's work. They used a computer graph drawing program to collate the data they had collected. Then they used the graphs to decide which are the most popular colours for front doors.

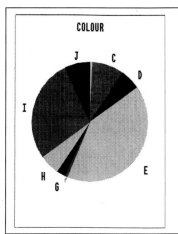

Name:	Number:
A Black	1
B Blue	0
C Brown	11
D Cream	7
E DG	52
F Green	1
G Orange	3
H Red	7
I White	35
J Yellow	9

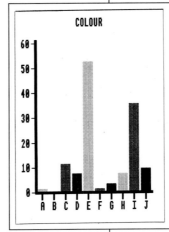

Name:	Number:
A Black	1
B Blue	0
C Brown	11
D Cream	7
E DG	52
F Green	1
G Orange	3
H Red	7
I White	35
J Yellow	9

3 How does colour influence our choice of food and drink?

Many children and their parents are becoming increasingly concerned about additives to our food and drink. Children could explore the ways in which we are influenced by the colour of what we eat and drink.

The colour wheel in *Light* could be useful for this activity.

Ask the children to think of food and drinks under different colour headings.

Q *How many purple foods can you think of?*
How many blue drinks can you think of?
How could you find out which colour other children prefer different foods to be?

The children could add food colouring to some mashed potato and offer this to their friends.

PLANNING AND CARRYING OUT FAIR TESTS

TAKE CARE OVER HYGIENE

Q *Which colours do your friends prefer to try?*
Which colours do they refuse to try?
Does the colour of food and drink affect the flavour?
Can you think how to test this idea? Is it a fair test?

A group of children could add common 'drink colours' to some sparkling mineral water or lemonade. They could ask another group of children to guess the flavour of the drinks. This will help them to decide whether the colour of the drink really affects the flavour, or whether we assume a flavour is there because we have learnt by experience that certain colours are associated with certain flavours.

SOME CHILDREN ARE THOUGHT TO REACT ADVERSELY TO TARTRAZINE (E102 – A RED COLOUR, ALSO USED MIXED WITH OTHER COLOURS); FOOD COLOUR WITHOUT TARTRAZINE CAN BE OBTAINED FROM HEALTH FOOD SHOPS

3.3

AT 1 INTERPRETING RESULTS AND FINDINGS

t SUGGEST THAT CHILDREN MIX FOOD COLOURS IF YOU HAVE A LIMITED RANGE – MAKE SURE THE TASTING GROUPS DON'T SEE THE DRINKS BEING PREPARED, OR SEE ONE ANOTHER'S TESTS

v

Another group of children could act as a control by trying the same test blindfolded with careful supervision.

Q *Is it so easy to guess the flavour of food or drink when you cannot see what you are eating or drinking?*

Ask the children to think about the implications of their findings.

Q *Do we really need food colouring? If so, why?*

4 Coloured filters

Children may have heard the expression 'looking at the world through rose-tinted spectacles'. Ask them:

Q *What do you think this expression means?*
What will happen if we look at the world through different-coloured glasses?

The children could predict what will happen if they look through acetate of different colours.

Q *What effect will it have on the colours around us?*
What kind of 'mood' do colours create?
Which colours create a cold/warm/mysterious feel?

More about light includes a poem about a child's feelings about colours.

 pb

The children could make a diorama using some models, a shoe box and some coloured acetate. Which colour would they choose for their dinosaur world, moonscape or magic kingdom?

 e

Q *Why do people sometimes wear dark glasses?*

The children could try making their own dark-coloured glasses to find out what effects are produced.

5 Mixing colours

a Mixing paints

(See page 79 for the distinction between filters and paints.) Ask the children:

Q *If you had only (e.g.) red and blue paints, do you think you could mix them to make (e.g.) purple?*

AT
1   HYPOTHESIZING.
PREDICTING

Most children will already have had experience of mixing coloured paints. They could use this as an opportunity to predict and then to test their ideas. Ask, for example:

Q *What colour will you get if you mix equal amounts of blue and green paint?*

Get the children to record their results in two columns headed 'What I expected' and 'What happened'.

Give the children a limited choice of colours to paint a picture with, possibly only two colours. Different children in the class could try different combinations of colours.

Q *Which colours are the most useful when it comes to mixing colours?*

AT
1   INTERPRETING RESULTS
AND FINDINGS

If you increase the choice to three colours, what difference does this make to the range of colours you can mix?

b Colour spinners

Q *What do you think will happen if you make a spinner made of (e.g.) red and blue?*

AT
1   PREDICTING

Give the children the opportunity to make a variety of spinners, predicting first what the outcome will be.

Q *Can you make a green spinner by using three colours?*

Try this with other combinations, including black and white.

More about light gives examples of dot pictures which produce a mixing effect.

CHAPTER 4 — Assessment

4.1 Introduction

You will have been assessing your children's ideas and skills by using the activities in this teachers' guide. This on-going, formative assessment is essentially part of teaching since what you find is immediately used in suggesting the next steps to help the children's progress. But this information can also be brought together and summarized for purposes of recording and reporting progress. This summary of performance has to be in terms of National Curriculum level descriptions at the end of the key stages, and some schools keep records in terms of levels at other times.

This chapter helps you summarize the information you have from children's work in terms of level descriptions. Examples of work relating to the theme of this guide are discussed and features which indicate activity at a certain level are pointed out to show what to look for in your pupils' work as evidence of achievement at one level or another. It is necessary, however, to look across the full range of work, and not judge from any single event or piece of work.

There are two sets of examples provided. The first is the assessment of skills in the context of the activities related to the concepts covered in this guide. The second deals with the development of these concepts.

4.2 Assessment of skills (AT1)

Things to look for when pupils are investigating light, as indicating progress from level 2 to level 5:

Level 2: Making suggestions as well as responding to others' suggestions about how to find things out about light, such as what it will pass through. Using equipment, such as mirrors, magnifying glasses and transparent, translucent, and opaque materials, to make observations. Recording what they find and comparing it with what they expected.

Level 3: Saying what they expect to happen when something is changed and suggesting ways of collecting information to test their predictions. Carrying out fair tests, knowing why they are fair, and making measurements. Recording what they find in a variety of ways; noticing any patterns in it.

Level 4: Making predictions which guide the planning of fair tests. Using suitable equipment and making adequate and relevant observations. Using tables and charts to record measurements and other observations. Interpreting, drawing conclusions and attempting to relate findings to scientific knowledge.

Level 5: Planning controlled investigations of predictions which are based on scientific knowledge. Using equipment carefully, repeating observations as necessary. Using line graphs to record and help interpretation; considering findings in relation to scientific knowledge.

Zoe, Gareth and Shiraz talked about warning signals and signs. They discussed the sounds, symbols and colours used, and the need to make warning signs clearly visible.

The teacher provided the children with sheets of coloured paper, coloured pencils and pens, and asked them to design their own warning signs.

The children decided to make a sign warning 'DANGER – SCHOOL', and chose bright pink paper for the background.

The teacher asked:

How could you find out which colours show up well on your paper?

The children discussed the question. They thought of writing 'DANGER' in different colours and then said:

> *Looking at them.*
>
> *Looking through the back of the paper.*
>
> *Holding them up so you can see.*

They each decided on a colour and began writing 'DANGER'. Zoe suggested that they could compare the colours by using the letter D on its own. This suggestion was accepted by Gareth and Shiraz.

The teacher asked the children to write down what they were going to do.

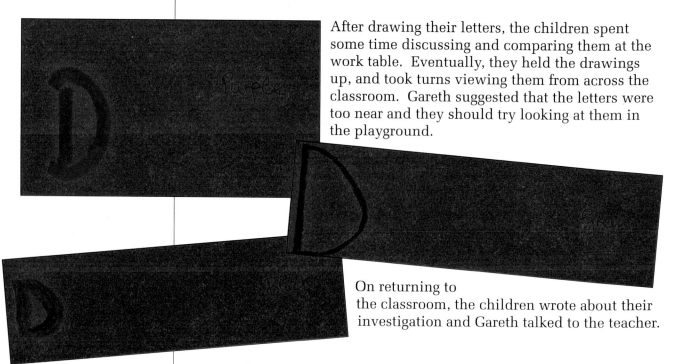

After drawing their letters, the children spent some time discussing and comparing them at the work table. Eventually, they held the drawings up, and took turns viewing them from across the classroom. Gareth suggested that the letters were too near and they should try looking at them in the playground.

On returning to the classroom, the children wrote about their investigation and Gareth talked to the teacher.

The teacher asked the children:

Are there any other reasons why the purple letter is clearer than the black and green letter?

I'm going to test diffrent colours on pink paper. To see what colour shows the best. The colour we have chosen is purple green & black. I wrote the letter D in purple. on a luminous pink piece of paper. and then we tested them in the science room. But we could see them clearly in the room. So we went out in to the playground and put the pieces of paper on the fence and went to the other end of the playground. But we couldn't see anything, we could only see pink paper on the fence, So we walked half the playground. We saw purple and the black letter and then green, I thougth it was going to be black

Zoe

I'm going test different clours on pink paper. The clours we have chosen are black green and purple. W: wrote the letter D in black on a luminous pink paper. Then we tested it in the science room. Then we decided to go into the playground We put them on the fence then we went up to about the shed then we could'int see nouthing then we decided wich one was best. And this is wot we came up with 1st was purple 2nd was black 3rd was green

Shiraz

I'm going to test diffrent cders on pink papper To see what coler shows up best! We chosen green puple black<
I Wrote D on a pink Peice off paper With green.

Gareth

Gareth thought there were no other reasons. Shiraz suggested that the purple letter was clear because it was in felt-tip. Zoe said the test was fair because they had used a letter D for each colour.

Finally, in this investigation the children looked back at their work and thought of ways of improving it.

Gareth	We tested to see if we could see it by going far away from it. We decided to go outside and test. We stuck them onto the gate and walked back to see which one was the best.
Teacher	How did you know which one was the best?
Gareth	We knew which one was the best because we could see it further back than the others. The black was second best because it was the second one I could see the best, the green was next best, then the black.
Teacher	Which colour will you use on your sign?
Gareth	I would use the purple to write the sign.
Teacher	Why would you use this?
Gareth	Because I can see it best.

All three children made suggestions about what they wanted to find out and how they were going to do it. They carried out their investigation, recorded what they did and interpreted their results in terms of their expectations. Thus their work fully meets the requirements at level 2 and goes beyond this in several respects. We therefore consider it in relation to the description of level 3.

Zoe and Shiraz explain how the test was planned and why the location had to be changed. This shows a clear grasp of what they were finding out. Gareth's account is not so clear in this respect. In their own terms they tested the signs fairly, by writing the same letter on each, putting them in the same position and carrying out the same process in judging them. Although other aspects were not controlled (the type of pen used and the size of the letters) the work shows an awareness of the need for fair testing, which with other evidence indicates achievement at level 3. They did not make measurements, but in their plan, comparison of the distances at which the signs could be seen was quite adequate.

In all cases they interpreted their findings consistently with the evidence and, even though Gareth's account is less detailed, he drew conclusions from the results in discussion with the teacher. All the children could be helped to make progress in their investigation skills, and in presenting their findings in appropriate ways. The refinement of fair testing and the introduction of quantification could arise from discussion with other children.

4.3 Assessment of children's understanding (Part of AT4)

Aspects of work on light which indicates levels 2 to 5:

Level 2: Knowing that light passes through some materials but not others, that darkness is the absence of light . Distinguishing between sources of light and reflection from shiny surfaces.

Level 3: Realizing that light is reflected from surfaces and how reflection differs from transmission.

Level 4: Awareness that light travels from its source at very high speed and that this can be represented by straight lines. Using this idea to explain the shape of shadows.

Level 5: Pupils realizing that we see an object when light from it enters our eyes.

Steven

As part of a discussion of light passing through some materials and not others, Steven and Dirk were asked to explain the conditions in which a shadow is formed. Steven shows an awareness of sunlight travelling by describing it as a beam. He also generalizes about the type of object that casts a shadow as one through which light does not pass, showing knowledge of such materials.

Compared with Steven, Dirk shows a greater understanding of what happens when a shadow is formed. His work appears to indicate awareness of light being reflected at the surface of the object and is at level 3 in this respect.

Steven's drawing shows some indication of the shape of the shadow, but not as clearly as the drawing of shadows given on page 60. In those cases there are sharp outlines and the shadows are in appropriate positions in relation to the Sun. This could be the result of careful observation but it might also indicate awareness that light travels in straight lines so that an object casts a shadow round its outline. If this were confirmed in discussion with the children it would indicate work at level 4.

A shadow happens when someone or something blocks the beam of the sun.

Dirk

a shadow is something when the sun's light bems down on us. because we ar opack the light dose not go throw us it corseis the light to bounco of us with means that the rest of ~~us~~ the light goes past

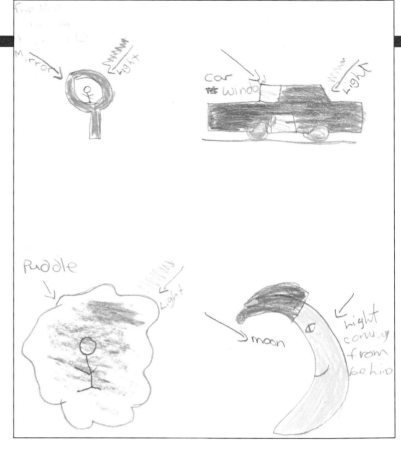

Farihah

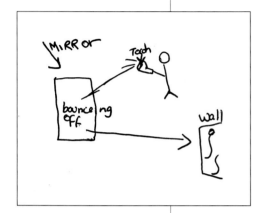

Farihah and Sabah have shown some places where light is reflected and their work in clearly at level 3. The majority of their examples show mirror surfaces and polished surfaces. Generally, the children are aware of light being reflected at these types of surfaces, and find the reflection of light on dull surfaces more of a problem. Some children may be unable to offer such a range of examples of reflections as Farihah and Sabah at level 3.

Sabah

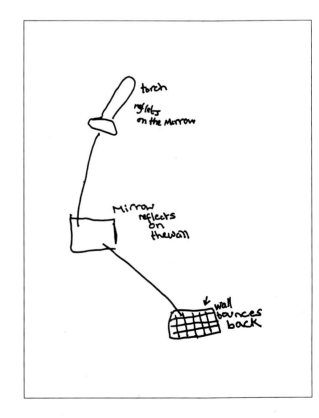

Keith and Sophia have shown how to send a beam of light around a corner to a friend. In each of these drawings, the light is shown travelling in straight lines. The children also appear to be aware of how light reflects from a surface. These aspects of the drawings would set the work above level 3.

Sophia

Silvia, Khilno and George were asked to show in their drawing how they see objects. Silvia's representation of light suggests that the book is seen because light is reflected to the eye. This work appears to be at level 5.

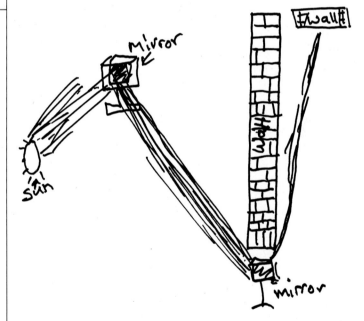

Keith

Silvia

George

The light shines on the clock so they can see. The Sun goes through the window so they can see. The table and chair could be shining. They look with their eyes.

Khilno

Khilno drew on a copiable sheet similar to the one on page 35. From his drawing alone it might appear that the children in the picture see the clock by reflection. However, his explanation indicates that the lines connecting the children to the clock illustrate them 'seeing' the clock by 'looking' at it, an idea of active vision. This idea of active vision may also explain George's illustration of how he sees a book.

Thus, some children's illustrations of how they see objects can be misleading, and teachers may need to ask children to explain their drawings.

When children come to consider how they see objects in different situations, their explanation may appear to be inconsistent. For example, consider Rega's drawing, which illustrates how she sees a card and a book. The card is illuminated by a torch.

Rega

Perhaps helped by the presence of the torch, Rega shows light reflected to the eye; with the book, in the absence of an obvious primary source, she may be resorting to the idea of active vision, and she connects the observer and the book. Therefore, at this level, children may need to show how they see an object both in the presence and absence of an obvious primary source.

CHAPTER 5

Background science

Where does light comes from?

Light is given off by atoms of matter which have been 'excited' – that is, some energy has been given to them. The energy is generally provided either by heating or by passing electricity at a high voltage through a gas. The former is what happens in a normal light bulb and the Sun, while the latter is what happens in fluorescent lamps and advertising signs.

An advantage of fluorescent lamps is that less energy is needed to produce the light, so these appliances are cheaper to run. Also, because the light comes from a long tube, it is more diffuse – that is, spread out – than light from a small bulb, so it gives a softer effect, without hard shadows. Some modern energy-saving lights are fluorescent tubes folded into the compact space of a bulb.

How fast does light travel?

DO NOT LOOK DIRECTLY AT THE SUN

Light travels very, very quickly – at 300,000 km per second (186,000 miles per second). Even at this speed, light from the Sun takes 8 minutes to reach Earth. This means that when we look at the Sun the light entering our eye set out 8 minutes ago, so we are seeing the Sun not as it is now but as it was 8 minutes ago. In the case of the next nearest star, light takes 4 years to reach us. However, it is very difficult to show that light does take a finite time to travel. This is because light travels so fast that it is impossible to see it moving. When you turn on the light, the effect is instantaneous and you do not notice light going from the bulb to the four corners of the room.

This often means that it is difficult for children to build an idea that light travels and many of them regard light as something which is just there – 'filling' or 'flooding'– a room. All you can do is show that light can be used to 'send' messages, for example, by signalling with a torch. The message travels, so it follows that the light must be travelling too. In fact light is used to carry messages in modern telephone systems. Instead of electricity in wires, these have light travelling along fine glass fibres. The light signal is turned into electricity to work the telephone.

How does light travel?

Light travels in straight lines unless it is deflected. One piece of evidence for this can be seen when you look at the light from a projector, a spotlight or a bright torch. If chalk dust or talc is scattered into the beam, the path of the light can be seen.

The other principal piece of evidence comes from shadows. The shadows produced on a wall by your hand, or your shadow on a bright sunny day, have fairly sharp edges. If light travelled in curved lines, it would bend around your body or hand so that the edge of the shadow would be more diffuse.

Evidence that light travels in a straight line

Light from a laser is the best example of light travelling in straight lines, though unfortunately it is often unavailable to schools. Here the light can be seen travelling over very long distances in a straight line. More definite proof can be obtained by taking three cards with holes through their centres and lining them up so that you can see a bulb on the far side of the first one. If the cards are held in position, for instance with Plasticine, a piece of cotton thread can be passed through the holes. Pulling the cotton thread taut shows the path travelled by the ray of light is a straight line. (This is not an experiment to do with children as the point it is making is not self-evident.)

Looked at closely, the light from an ordinary torch bulb, particularly in a semi-darkened room, does seem to be coming out in a spray of lines. When they are given such an activity as an observation task, many children will remark on this feature, and most of their drawings of light sources show lines like these. This observation could be used to support the idea that light travels in lines. Although it is, unfortunately, an optical illusion created when the light from the filament (the tiny wire inside the bulb) passes through the glass, children do not know this; for once, it is a helpful effect which lends some support to the idea we hope they develop.

'Rays of light' coming from a simple bulb

What is colour?

Light, like sound and radio signals, travels in waves. Like these, it too has a wavelength. We see light of different wavelengths as having different colours. The colours of the rainbow – red, orange, yellow, green, blue, indigo and violet – are in order of decreasing wavelength. (It is difficult – or impossible – to distinguish the indigo.)

If we see light of a single wavelength, we see a single colour, for example, yellow. But if we see a mixture of red and green light, we also experience this as yellow. This is caused by the human eye, not by the nature of light. A machine could tell the difference.

Mixing coloured light

There are three colours of light which can be mixed to make any other bright colour. These are red, green and blue. They are called the **primary** colours. The picture on a colour television screen consists simply of red, blue and green dots or small stripes. Note that they make other colours by being added together, for example by shining two spots of coloured light on to the same place on a screen. This is called colour mixing **by addition**. Red, green and blue are the **additive primary colours**.

If you add the three primary colours in the right proportions you see white light. The white light from the Sun includes all the colours from red to violet. When sunlight falls on yellow paint, the primary colours of red and green light are reflected back from it. All the other colours are absorbed by the paint. When sunlight falls on blue paint, blue is reflected and other colours absorbed.

Mixing coloured paint

This is a different kind of colour mixing: mixing by **subtraction**, because the mixing reduces the range of colour that is reflected. Subtractive colour mixing also has three primary colours, which can be mixed to give any other colour though the mixture is always a darker shade than the original paints. The **subtractive primary colours** are magenta (blue–red), yellow, and cyan (blue–green), loosely referred to as red, yellow and blue. This is the kind of colour mixing that children are familiar with. If you mix blue with yellow paint, the mixture absorbs all the colours absorbed by each of the paints. Cyan absorbs all colours but blue and green, yellow all colours but red and green, so green is the only colour not absorbed and hence the colour of the mixture.

Splitting white light

White light can be split up into the colours it is made of. This can be done with a prism, and happens naturally in raindrops to make a rainbow. When light passes from air to glass or water and back into air, it is *refracted* – roughly, bent. Different colours are bent to different angles, so the light spreads out into a *spectrum* or rainbow.

How do colour filters work?

Colour filters do what their name implies, that is, remove colour from white light. White light viewed through a red filter looks red because the filter allows colours at the red end of the spectrum to pass, but stops the other colours.

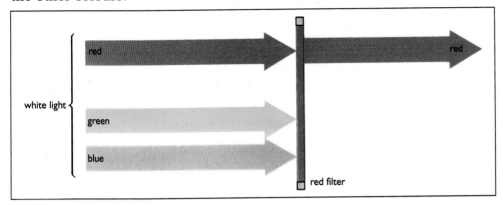

The effect of a colour filter on white light

Children intuitively explain filters differently: they generally think that the red filter 'adds' colour to the white light. It can be difficult to convince them that the opposite of this explanation is the truth, that the filter removes colours. A convincing explanation for adults is to look at white light through any two colour filters. If the first filter is red, it lets through only red light which the second filter, either a blue or green one, will not let pass. The result is that no light passes; it is virtually obscured by the two filters. (However, the filters do need to be relatively pure filters for this to be convincing. Normal cheap filters let through a broad band of colours.)

Sharp shadow cast by a point source

What are shadows?

Shadows are caused by objects that are opaque – that is, they do not allow light to pass through them. On a sunny day you can clearly see a shadow of yourself on the ground. Because your body is opaque, the light that hits it from behind does not reach the ground in front of you. As a result, this part of the ground appears darker to your eye than the surrounding ground which is receiving the full sunlight. It is not actually dark (in the sense that no light is reaching the area), as some light scattered off other surrounding objects still reaches this part of the ground. If you look closely, objects and detail can be seen in the shadow; it just appears darker to the eye, so it looks black. As you move, your body blocks out a different section of the ground and your shadow moves with you.

Why aren't all shadows sharp?

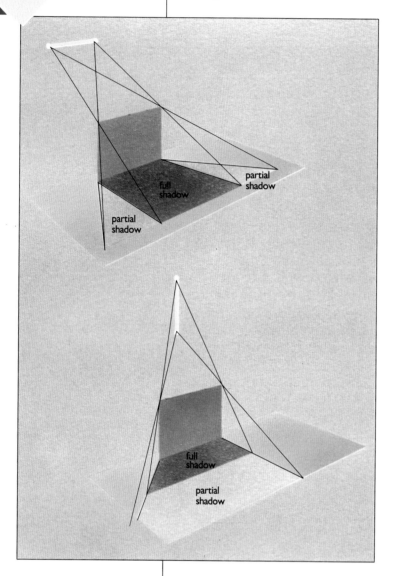

Some lights, however, do not make sharp shadows. Fluorescent lamps, which produce their light from a long glass tube, are an extended source of light. Even if the light from one part of the lamp is blocked off, the path of light from another part of the lamp is not obscured and the light is able to partially fill in the shadow. The result is that shadows made by fluorescent lamps are very soft and lack sharp edges. The lighting is much more even, and does not create glare. However, it does not light any one area very brightly, so you might still need a conventional lamp to light your desk, for example.

Why are there no shadows on cloudy days?

The Sun's light is scattered and spread out on its way through the atmosphere – which is why a clear daytime sky looks bright blue, not black. (The reason for it being blue is discussed later.) On a cloudy day, sunlight hitting the clouds is scattered in all directions. Since the light reaches the ground from many different directions, there are no shadows.

Shadows formed by extended sources of light

In the theatre, a single compact bright light source is used to create strong shadows. To produce a soft lighting effect, lights are spread over a wide angle.

What happens when light hits an object?

Much of the behaviour of light can be explained by what happens when it hits an object.

The simplest object to consider is a mirror. Mirrors consist of shiny metal surfaces. A glass mirror has a thin coating of aluminium on the back and it is this thin coating, not the glass, which reflects most of the light. Very simply, when light hits the mirror it bounces off, and this is called reflecting. Polished metal surfaces are very good reflectors, reflecting over 95 per cent of the light which hits them.

Light which goes straight on to the mirror (that is, at 90°) is reflected straight back. But if light shines on to the mirror at any other angle it will not be reflected straight back, but will bounce away from the mirror at the same angle as it hit the mirror. The scientific way of describing this is to say that the angle of incidence equals the angle of reflection. A good practical model is that of a ball hitting a wall. Thrown straight at the wall, it comes straight back. Thrown on at an angle, the ball comes off at the same angle as that at which it hit the wall.

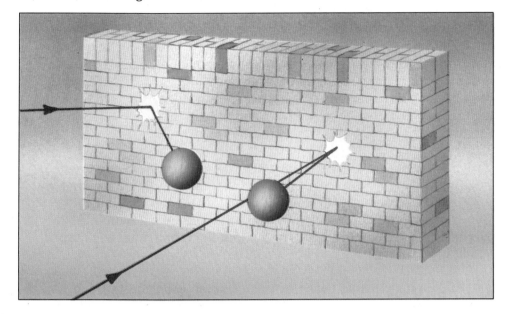

Model of light hitting a mirror

Although the explanation of reflection may seem simple, it is an important idea to grasp; it is, for example, used by teachers in secondary schools to explain how we manage to see an image of ourselves in the mirror. Children make use of the idea to bounce sunlight off mirrors into people's eyes. This irritating habit should be discouraged as the sun is an extremely powerful light source and looking at it directly can damage the eyes. More appropriate uses of mirrors are for looking behind you, as in the driving mirror of a car, and looking around corners or over objects with a periscope.

Rougher surfaces reflect light in a more random, diffuse way and do not give images. Whether something gives a reflected image depends on how well the light is reflected from it, not on the amount of light reflected. White paper reflects more light than black glass, but only the latter gives a reflected image.

White light hitting a red object

When light is reflected from an object whose surface is too rough to give a mirror image, it spreads out in all directions. The surface of the object, therefore, looks the same from all angles – in contrast to a mirror, where the surface looks different when seen from different angles.

When white light hits an opaque object, if all the colours in the white light are reflected it looks white. Many materials absorb some colours of light and reflect others. To our eyes, these materials look coloured. An object that absorbs most of the light at the violet end of the spectrum, and reflects most of the light at the red end, looks red. If the object absorbs all colours of light it looks black. Light that is absorbed is not lost. It is absorbed and warms the object. That is why black objects get so hot in strong sunlight, while white ones stay fairly cool. Mirrors stay coolest of all. But all objects, even mirrors, absorb some light.

Unfortunately there are no simple proofs of these ideas.

Most children think that when light hits an object or a piece of paper the light is stopped. The evidence to contradict this is limited. Some thought using commonsense reasoning shows that this would explain why white rooms appear so bright. The white walls absorb almost no light and the light is bounced around the room.

However, it is possible to deal with the commonsense idea that when white light hits a coloured object, the object *adds* red light to what we see instead of removing other colours. If a white object is placed next to a coloured one, the white one looks brighter. An object which looks brighter is reflecting more light, so the red object must have absorbed some light.

Light, of course, can also pass through some objects, and these are said to be transparent or translucent. The word 'transparent' is usually restricted to a material which allows light to pass straight through it, so that we can see through it. Materials which allow only a little light to pass through them, or which reflect or bend the path of the light in a disorderly way as it goes through, are described as translucent. Many plastics are translucent. If a material allows quite a lot of light through, but muddles its path so that no clear image can be seen through it, it is usually called translucent. A thin white plastic bag may let more light through it than a sheet of blue glass; but the first is called translucent and the second transparent.

Transparent objects can also change the direction of light. This occurs when the beam passes from one transparent material into another, for example from air into glass or water. A scientific explanation of refraction is too complex for children at this stage, but it can simply be called 'bending'.

How do we see objects?

Many people believe that we see with our eyes actively, and that our eyes give off some kind of sight rays which select the object of our attention. Even our language reflects this idea: we 'look daggers', 'cast our gaze', 'peer through' and 'catch their eyes'.

The scientific understanding is the exact opposite of this. We see objects because light from the objects *enters our eyes*. There are no rays which leave our eyes. Our eyes are active only in the sense that we have to direct our vision to the point of interest, and that our eyes form an image on the retina of the light that goes into them.

Clearly most people will agree that we need light to see with. However, the common assumption referred to above – that we see because rays emanate from our eyes – does not stand up to close examination. If this were the case, why is it that when the light is low we see objects only dimly? If rays were coming out of our eyes, seeing would not depend on the amount of light present; we would be able to see whether there was light around or not. Some children attempt to get round this problem by showing light going from a source to the eye and then to the object. This would explain why we need light to see by and why we do not see so well when it gets dark. It is an interesting attempt to be logical and consistent. However, if you shroud your eyes with your hands to reduce the amount of light falling on your eyes, you still see objects in the room just as brightly. Clearly, this is because there is just as much light entering the eye from the object you are looking at through the gap in your hands.

Convincing children of this is not easy, as there is little concrete evidence to show how light travels. A good starting point is to use a torch and a mirror to 'bounce' the light from the torch via the mirror into someone's eyes. The light is clearly coming out of the torch and going to the mirror. Many children will also accept that the light is 'bouncing off' the mirror into their eyes. A grasp of this is possibly the best starting point for an understanding of how we see. Dust appearing in a beam of sunlight can now be explained as lots of tiny mirrors 'bouncing' light into the eye.

It is also interesting to observe what happens to the pupil of the eye when you go from a brightly lit room to a dark room. The iris (the coloured part of the eye) opens out and the pupil (the dark central circle) gets bigger. Going from a dull room to a bright room produces the opposite effect. This is the eye's way of controlling the amount of light entering it so that the retina – the light–sensitive part – is not damaged. However, this explanation is understandable only if you believe that light enters the eye when you see something. People who believe that rays come out of the eye will find difficulty reconciling their theory with this observation.

Scattering of light by air molecules

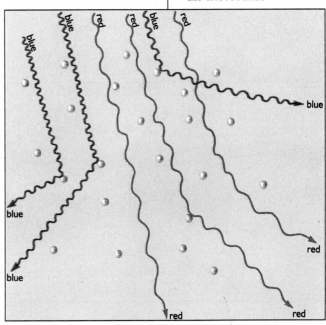

If this observation is used as a focus of discussion with children, a further point of interest will emerge if a child points out that cat's eyes 'glow' in the dark. Cats' eyes glow only when light, such as the beam of car headlamps, hits them, and not otherwise. The reason is that the retina of a cat is partially reflective and some of the light entering the eye bounces back, so that light is actually coming out of the cat's eye as well as going in. However, the cat is seeing by the light that enters its eye.

Children often ask why the sky is blue. The answer is hard for them to grasp. As sunlight passes through the atmosphere it has to pass the molecules of the air and water vapour. Light from the violet end of the spectrum, which has shorter wavelengths, is more easily scattered by these molecules, so more of it is turned aside and spreads out at all angles. This scattered light, a mixture of violet, blue and green, looks blue. The light which gets straight through retains more colour from the red end of the spectrum, so that the Sun seems to have a yellowish colour.

When the Sun is low in the sky, its light goes through the atmosphere towards us at a low angle, so its path through the air is longer. More blue light is scattered, so the Sun looks redder.

Light in cameras

The simplest form of camera, a pinhole camera, relies on the fact that light travels in straight lines. When light reflected from an object passes through a small hole, the light coming from the top of the object goes through the hole at an angle which causes it to fall on the lower part of the light sensitive film inside the camera. The light from the bottom of the object falls on the upper part of the film. The same crossover occurs between the left and right sides of the object. The result is an image which reproduces the form of the object, but is reversed from top to bottom and side to side. However, all you need to do to get the image the right way round is to turn the film round (see the same figure, held upside down).

Principle of the pinhole camera

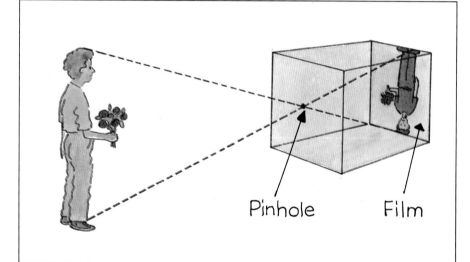

Pinhole   Film

A pinhole camera gives a good, sharp image, but the small hole does not let much light through. As a result, the time of the exposure has to be inconveniently long to allow a useful amount of light to fall on the film. A proper camera has a lens instead of a hole. This refracts the light to produce the same effect.

Wherever light from one part of the object strikes the lens, it will be refracted on to one part of the film. The diagram shows only a few of the infinite number of paths. The result is that the image thrown on to the film is bright, and will produce a picture in a fraction of a second.

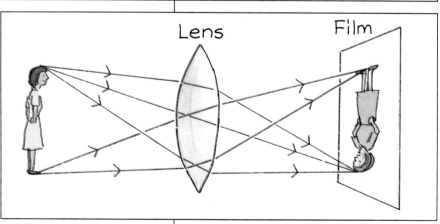

Lens   Film

Camera with a lens

Index

Trial schools

The SPACE Project and the Trust are grateful to the governors, staff, and pupils of all the trial schools. It will be obvious to readers of these guides how much we are indebted to them for their help, and especially for the children's drawn and written records of their hard work and their growing understanding of science.

All Saints Primary School, Barnet, Hertfordshire
Ansdell County Primary School, Lytham St Anne's, Lancashire
Bishop Endowed Church of England Junior School, Blackpool
Brindle Gregson Lane Primary School, Lancashire
Brookside Junior and Infants School, Knowsley
Chalgrove JMI School, Finchley, London N3
Christ the King Roman Catholic Primary School, Blackpool
English Martyrs Roman Catholic Primary School, Knowsley
Fairlie County Primary School, Skelmersdale, Lancashire
Fairway JMI School, Mill Hill, London NW7
Foulds Primary School, Barnet, Hertfordshire
Frenchwood County Primary School, Preston
Grange Park Primary School, London N21
Hallesville Primary School, Newham, London E6
Heathmore Primary School, Roehampton, London SW15
Honeywell Junior School, London SW11
Huyton Church of England Junior School, Knowsley
Longton Junior School, Preston
Mawdesley Church of England Primary School, Lancashire
Moor Park Infants School, Blackpool
Mosscroft County Primary School, Knowsley
Nightingale Primary School, London E18
Oakhill Primary School, Woodford Green, Essex
Park Brow County Primary School, Knowsley
Park View Junior School, Knowsley
Purford Green Junior School, Harlow, Essex
Ronald Ross Primary School, London SW19
Rosh Pinah School, Edgeware, Middlesex
Sacred Heart Junior School, Battersea, London SW11
St Aloysius Roman Catholic Infants School, Knowlsey
St Andrew's Roman Catholic Primary School, Knowsley
St Bernadette's Roman Catholic Primary School, Blackpool
St James's Church of England Junior School, Forest Gate, London E7
St John Fisher Roman Catholic Primary School, Knowsley
St John Vianney Roman Catholic Primary School, Blackpool
St Mary and St Benedict Roman Catholic Primary School, Bamber Bridge, Preston
St Peter and St Paul Roman Catholic Primary School, Knowsley
St Theresa's Roman Catholic Primary School, Blackpool
St Theresa's Roman Catholic Primary School, Finchley, London N3
Scarisbrick County Primary School, Lancashire
Selwyn Junior School, London E4
Snaresbrook Primary School, Wanstead, London E18
South Grove Primary School, Walthamstow, London E17
Southmead Infants School, London SW19
Staining Church of England Primary School, Blackpool
Walton-le-Dale County Primary School, Preston
West Vale County Primary School, Kirkby
Woodridge Primary School, North Finchley, London N12

NUFFIELD ◆ PRIMARY ◆ SCIENCE

INSPECTION COPY REQUEST AND ORDER FORM

Mrs/Ms/Miss/Mr:_____

Position:_____

School:_____

Address:_____

Postcode:_____ LEA:_____

Code 2113 (Sept 1995)

Please send me:

Title	ISBN	inspection copy	Order Quantity
Infant Teacher's Guides			
Electricity and Magnetism	0 00 310242 4	☐	_____
Living Processes	0 00 310243 2	☐	_____
Forces and Movement	0 00 310244 0	☐	_____
The Earth in Space	0 00 310245 9	☐	_____
Light	0 00 310246 7	☐	_____
Materials	0 00 310247 5	☐	_____
Rocks, Soil and Weather	0 00 310248 3	☐	_____
Sound and Music	0 00 310249 1	☐	_____
Using Energy	0 00 310250 5	☐	_____
The Variety of Life	0 00 310251 3	☐	_____
Living Things in Their Environment	0 00 310252 1	☐	_____
Junior Teacher's Guides			
The Earth in Space	0 00 310253 X	☐	_____
Electricity and Magnetism	0 00 310254 8	☐	_____
Forces and Movement	0 00 310255 6	☐	_____
Light	0 00 310256 4	☐	_____
Living Processes	0 00 310257 2	☐	_____
Living Things in Their Environment	0 00 310258 0	☐	_____
Materials	0 00 310259 9	☐	_____
Rocks, Soil and Weather	0 00 310260 2	☐	_____
Sound and Music	0 00 310261 0	☐	_____
Using Energy	0 00 310262 9	☐	_____
The Variety of Life	0 00 310263 7	☐	_____
Science Co-ordinator's Handbook	0 00 310089 8	☐	_____
In-Service Pack	0 00 310019 7	☐	_____
Infant Evaluation Pack	0 00 310091X	☐	_____
Junior Evaluation Pack	0 00 310090 1	☐	_____
Infant Pupils' Books			
A first look at time and space	0 00 310064 2	☐	_____
A first look at electricity and magnets	0 00 310067 7	☐	_____
A first look at moving things	0 00 310066 9	☐	_____
A first look at light	0 00 310068 5	☐	_____
A first look at living things	0 00 310059 6	☐	_____

Title	ISBN	inspection copy	Order Quantity
A first look at where things live	0 00 310061 8	☐	_____
A first look at what things are made of	0 00 310065 0	☐	_____
A first look at rocks, soil and weather	0 00 310073 1	☐	_____
A first look at sound and music	0 00 310069 3	☐	_____
A first look at energy	0 00 310063 4	☐	_____
A first look at different animals and plants	0 00 310060 X	☐	_____
Lower Junior Pupils' Books - Years 3-4			
Time and space	0 00 310042 1	☐	_____
Electricity and magnetism	0 00 310032 4	☐	_____
Forces and movement	0 00 310024 3	☐	_____
Light	0 00 310020 0	☐	_____
Living things in action	0 00 310036 7	☐	_____
Habitats	0 00 310040 5	☐	_____
Materials	0 00 310028 6	☐	_____
Rocks, soil and weather	0 00 310038 3	☐	_____
Sound and music	0 00 310022 7	☐	_____
Using energy	0 00 310030 8	☐	_____
Different plants and animals	0 00 310026 X	☐	_____
Upper Junior Pupils' Books - Years 5-6			
More about time and space	0 00 310043 X	☐	_____
More about electricity and magnetism	0 00 310033 2	☐	_____
More about forces and movement	0 00 310025 1	☐	_____
More about light	0 00 310021 9	☐	_____
More about living things in action	0 00 310037 5	☐	_____
More about habitats	0 00 310041 3	☐	_____
More about materials	0 00 310029 4	☐	_____
More about rocks, soil and weather	0 00 310039 1	☐	_____
More about sound and music	0 00 310023 5	☐	_____
More about using energy	0 00 310031 6	☐	_____
More about different plants and animals	0 00 310027 8	☐	_____
Total quantity			_____

HOW TO ORDER

 0141 306 3484   FAX 0141 306 3750   ✉ Collins Educational, HarperCollins Publishers, FREEPOST GW5078, Bishopbriggs, Glasgow G64 1BR

PLEASE PHOTOCOPY THIS PAGE